GEOPOLITICS FOR INVESTORS

Pippa Malmgren

CFA Institute
Research
Foundation

Statement of Purpose

The CFA Institute Research Foundation is a not-for-profit organization established to promote the development and dissemination of relevant research for investment practitioners worldwide.

ISBN 978-1-934667-83-5

3 March 2015

Editorial Staff

Stephen Smith
Editor

Pat Light
Assistant Editor

Cindy Maisannes
Manager, Publications Production

Christina Hampton
Publishing Technology Specialist

Biography

Philippa "Pippa" Malmgren is president and founder of the DRPM Group. Previously, she served as deputy head of global strategy at UBS and as chief currency strategist and head of global investment management business at Bankers Trust. Dr. Malmgren also served as a financial market adviser to US President George W. Bush, as a member of the National Economic Council, and as a member of the President's Working Group on Financial Markets and the Working Group on Corporate Governance. She serves on several advisory boards and working groups, including the British Ministry of Defence Working Group on Global Strategic Trends, the Greater London Authority Infrastructure Advisory Group, the MIT Legatum Center for Development and Entrepreneurship, and the Indiana University School of Public Policy and Environmental Affairs. Dr. Malmgren is a frequent guest on the BBC and a guest anchor for CNBC and Bloomberg. She holds a BA from Mount Vernon College and an MSc and a PhD from the London School of Economics.

Contents

CE Qualified Activity CFA Institute

This publication qualifies for 5 CE credits under the guidelines of the CFA Institute Continuing Education Program.

Foreword

When I qualified as a doctor, being a generalist was a common career option. Today, it seems as though more and more of my colleagues are specialising in ever more detailed and intricate areas of medicine. The same has been true of my experience in politics. The era of the generalist seems to be receding into the past, and the ability to see holistically is limited—not only by this particular phenomenon but also by an increase in political short-termism and a lack of institutional memory. Those who can remember high inflation, the effects of interest rate hikes, or even, in a European context, state control of prices and wages are increasingly rare. Fewer and fewer politicians can remember when the "Washington Consensus" was not the generally accepted creed for the governance of the global economy. Memories of the tensions and dangers of the Cold War are fading into the past, all too often being replaced by an irrational optimism that seems to lack logic and empiricism. Geopolitics today is moving markets but is dominated by wishful thinking rather than critical analysis. This matters in terms of our future security and prosperity, which is why Dr. Malmgren's analysis is both timely and important.

The world of globalisation and geopolitics, in which we currently find ourselves, brings both opportunities and risks that are new. Yet, the forces and values used in shaping it are not. Territorial acquisition, political and religious ideology, and economic doctrine are all still in play. We need only look at Russian aggression in Crimea, the barbarity of ISIS (or ISIL, the Islamic State of Iraq and the Levant) in the Middle East, and the challenges to economic orthodoxy that run from Greece to Venezuela to see ample examples of this fact.

The era of globalisation not only brings greater interdependence in terms of both the global economy and security but also makes it impossible to disaggregate risk in a way that might have been possible in the past. Our governmental structures, however, have not yet adjusted to this reality. Government by silo, with an inability to connect the dots, adds to the difficulties we face in managing risk down. Fund managers are similar, with their narrow focus on single asset classes and single countries.

If we are to succeed in this task, there are a number of things that we have to do. First, we have to understand the concept and application of risk and how to measure it. Second, we have to find mechanisms to manage it in real time, minimising the risk of quantum leaps resulting from unpredicted external events. In terms of policy, we have to understand that if we do not allow change, including geopolitical change, to be a process, it is likely to become a stream of destabilising events.

Crucial to this management of geopolitical risk is seeing how things really are, not how we would like them to be. Events that have come to be known as the Arab Spring are a good recent example. The uprisings in countries like Tunisia and Egypt were certainly stimulated by global food price spikes in 2008 and 2010, with the result that state subsidies were unable to prevent prices of staple commodities from rising to hitherto unknown heights. In democracies, we throw out failing governments. In autocracies, people take to the streets. Yet, such was the desire of Western politicians to see this as a spontaneous outburst of support for Western liberal, democratic values and institutions, that the fundamental point was lost. A market phenomenon, a price change, spurred the overthrow of a government. This point was missed, and confusion followed for policymakers and investors alike.

Understanding historical and cultural context, as well as the interrelations between different elements of risk in the global economy, is an essential tool in the management of today's world. Zero geopolitical risk is not a realisable goal. To fail to understand and address geopolitics and the various interconnected disciplines is to fail to exercise due diligence. Dr. Malmgren's work, Geopolitics for Investors, is an essential addition to the toolbox of those who seek to manage elements of global business, finance, and security. The CFA Institute Research Foundation was prescient in commissioning this work last year given all that has now unfolded. This book is a timely handrail. It will help readers consider *how* to think about geopolitics before they dive into *what* to think about geopolitics. Those who fail to understand and act upon its advice and lessons do so at their own risk.

Liam Fox
Member of UK Parliament for North Somerset
Former UK Secretary of State for Defence

1. How to Think about Geopolitics

Geopolitical issues have a profound effect on investment strategies and results. But there has been no easy-to-read and accessible guide to geopolitics for investors—until now.

Geopolitics is everywhere. In August 2014, US Secretary of Defense Chuck Hagel said, "The world is exploding all over."[1] Coups have occurred and juntas have come to power from Tunisia to Thailand. Social upheaval and civil unrest are becoming more widespread, with street protests and riots from Argentina and Brazil to South Africa and Asia. The "Arab Spring" continues to unfold throughout the Middle East and in other nations as well.

Geopolitical events in Ukraine have threatened the world's energy supply, the global food market, and the safety of commercial aviation, leading to Russia's departure from the G–8. In the South China Sea, the territorial disputes between China and its neighbors have become more militarily confrontational. Russia is challenging Japan more forcefully over the Kurile Islands and making incursions into US airspace.

The old fault lines of geopolitics have become unstable again. Both Russian and Chinese military vessels and aircraft are now frequently engaged in near misses and close confrontations with those of the United States and its allies. Allegations of nuclear missile launches, even if involving only unarmed missiles, remind us that nuclear and conventional weapons treaties that took a generation to negotiate can be violated or obliterated in the 2 to 60 minutes it takes an intercontinental ballistic missile (ICBM) to reach its target.

Separatist Movements

Everywhere we see the rise of separatist movements that threaten the territorial integrity of even the most important economies. The United Kingdom had the Scottish independence movement. The European Union faces the risk of exits by places as small as Catalonia and the city of Venice to countries as large as Greece and the United Kingdom. From the US state of California to Nigeria, more citizens are pushing for their preferred groups to gain greater autonomy from the existing government. National borders are under threat from multiple sources in multiple locales.

In the Middle East, the rise of civil strife in Syria and the return of conflict between Israel and Gaza signal a return to instability with global consequences. The United States' intended departure from the region

[1] Q&A with US Marines at Camp Pendleton, California, 13 August 2014.

(Afghanistan and Iraq) has begun to change allegiances and the balance of power there. Both Saudi Arabia and Israel are initiating diplomatic and commercial relationships with China and Russia as the United States' interest in their concerns seems to fade. Iran's influence in the region has increased, perhaps partly, but not only, because of its nuclear program. As a result, Saudi Arabia, Turkey, and even Egypt have all announced their intention to become nuclear powers. The nuclearisation of the Middle East is a new geopolitical development. Investors will have to decide whether it is going to be anything like the "mutual assured destruction" (MAD) approach that kept the United States and the Soviet Union in check during the Cold War era.

Borders Dissolving

The sudden disintegration of the long-established borders in the Middle East—from the era of the Sykes–Picot Agreement (1915)—is mirrored in other territories. Even the United States has had to deploy the National Guard in an effort to control its southern border, which has become porous as a result of immigration. China and India are increasingly arguing about the Line of Actual Control (LAC) between them, and both are building up troops and infrastructure and testing each other's resolve. Seemingly secure borders are becoming more vulnerable and fluid.

US relations with long-standing allies are under threat. Germany recently expelled the CIA's station chief in Berlin. Germany not only declined the United States' offer to join the "Five Eyes" intelligence network but also announced that the BND, Germany's intelligence agency, would begin spying on the United States. The whole purpose of the US military presence in Western Europe and NATO (North Atlantic Treaty Organization) is to protect Germany and Western Europe from Russia. Although the United States and Germany may have been spying on each other for years, publicly announcing that fact makes things awkward.

Core relationships that have underpinned the "world order" for decades seem to be deteriorating. France and Germany no longer see eye to eye, especially on economic and debt issues. The shared concerns of Germany and the rest of the EU no longer outweigh Germany's concern about the debt and structural problems elsewhere in the EU. Germany's desire for other eurozone members to delegate a higher degree of sovereignty over fiscal matters to Brussels has been met with political opposition in every eurozone nation that has had the opportunity to test the notion at the ballot box. The relationship between Russia and its border states has shifted from a benign to a challenging one. Russian border incursions into neighboring Baltic states and Ukraine have become commonplace. As a result, military forces from Sweden to the Balkans are enhancing their preparedness.

The United States' relationship with both China and Russia had been dominated by the assumption that common interests were more powerful than opposing interests. This understanding no longer seems to be the case. US, Russian, and Chinese military planes and vessels increasingly spar over international waters.

The many near misses between US spy planes and Chinese and Russian fighter jets are clear evidence that geopolitical risk should be an important topic for investors. Superpowers that can project their might into space are constantly testing and threatening each other's space-based capabilities. The desire for satellite and space dominance reveals how very important this ambition is both militarily and strategically in a world of high-tech communications.

Financial Architecture Questioned

Meanwhile, China and Russia are working together to create an alternative financial architecture for the world economy, and both countries increasingly challenge the United States and NATO militarily. The post–World War II order is embedded in institutions that have an uncertain role in today's world or that are often impotent to fulfil it, including the International Monetary Fund (IMF), the World Bank, NATO, the G–7/G–8/G–20, and the UN, among others. The fundamental principles that underpin the world economy and global markets are now increasingly called into question: Will or should the US dollar remain the world's reserve currency? China and Russia have spearheaded the creation of the BRIC Bank, the increased use of rubles and yuan in pricing and trading commodities, and a pooling of reserves for protection against a US dollar devaluation.

Non-State Actors

Many non-state actors are now at least as well equipped with technology and weapons as many nation-states. The Islamic State of Iraq and the Levant (ISIL or ISIS) can declare a caliphate in Iraq and take control of large swaths of territory. The pro-Russian separatists in Ukraine can bring down a commercial airliner with surprising accuracy. Terrorist groups can attack locations across the globe and enter the heart of their opponent's territory. Organised crime and commercial enterprises can be deeply affiliated with nation-states, making it possible for these states to use them in the conduct of statecraft without having to "own" the outcome. In other cases, such as Mexico's drug cartels or Eastern Europe's infamous cyberwarfare gangs, organised crime syndicates can operate entirely independently of the government and survive all efforts to shut them down.

Debt Problems

The fact that most major economies—from the United States to Europe to Japan—are heavily burdened by debt or financial difficulties makes the pursuit of military action less of an option. Ironically, their inability or unwillingness to deploy military strategies is arguably also spurring the return of geopolitics to the investment landscape. The lack of a credible committed defense attracts, if not invites, other nations to test borders and diplomatic boundaries.

In addition, the lack of reliable finance creates the impetus for higher taxation and regulation, which can undermine the relationships between citizens and their states. The "social contract" is increasingly questioned and challenged across both the industrialised world and the emerging markets as people realise that states cannot deliver on the promises they have made to their citizens. In the industrialised world, this dynamic puts pressure on existing geopolitical relationships. It not only stimulates separatist movements but also puts enormous pressure on the relationship that has been considered the linchpin of the European Union, that between Germany and France. The pressures of weak finances and weak growth seem to be dissolving the very glue that has traditionally held Europe together.

Financial distress is also what stimulates governments to reach for privately held assets, at home and abroad, whether held by citizens or noncitizens. Investors need to take particular care when considering the multitude of ways in which this can happen—from price controls to ownership restrictions to outright expropriation and confiscation. As we shall see, all these risks are geopolitical and can affect domestic and nondomestic investors alike.

2. What Is Geopolitics?

Why consider geopolitics when making investment decisions? In the end, the purpose of making an investment is not only to get your money back but also to make the best return possible, given the risks and opportunities involved. Therefore, investors who fail to consider all these factors could be shortchanging themselves and the interests of the capital for which they have a fiduciary responsibility. The deep interconnectedness of the world economy has caused high global correlations to be commonplace. Events abroad can easily affect purely domestic investment strategies. Most investment decisions must be assessed against the backdrop of alternative possible investments and locations, so a global perspective is necessary even when managing a purely domestic portfolio.

Defining Geopolitics

The following definition permits an assessment of the modern landscape of risk: Geopolitics generally refers to a state's projection of power abroad by any means or tools of statecraft. This definition encompasses both the active effort to engage in geopolitics in order to project power externally and the passive effort to respond to the geopolitical efforts of others to project power. It also encompasses all aspects of sovereignty and power, regardless of whether the tool or the objective is economic or political. The word "generally" is important because it leaves the door open to external non-state actors that increasingly are both the source of geopolitical pressures on states and the object of geopolitical efforts by states.

Risk is probably best described by Elroy Dimson, a professor at the London Business School: "Risk means more things can happen than will happen." When we combine the two topics—geopolitics and risk—we can say that *geopolitical risk* refers to the range of things that can happen that are caused by the efforts of states to project power. Investors and fund managers are principally interested in the market and economic consequences of geopolitical risk—that is, its effect on asset prices, although social, political, and legal issues can all affect valuations and prices as well. Culture and politics play their part in driving geopolitics, but geopolitics is about power projection aimed at multiple goals.

There are other definitions, but their usefulness for investors may be limited. The Merriam-Webster dictionary says:

> Geopolitics is the study of how geography and economics have an influence on politics and on the relations between nations and a study of the influence of such factors as geography, economics, and demography on the politics and especially the foreign policy of a state.

Encyclopaedia Britannica defines geopolitics as the "analysis of the geographic influences on power relationships in international relations."

Geopolitics is more than just foreign policy. It is one thing to consider nations' efforts to engage in international relations, which implies a series of bilateral relationships and dialogues. Geopolitics, in contrast, is a more inclusive term that speaks to the need to respond to the foreign policy of others as well as the vulnerability to events that are entirely outside national control. International relations does not really deal with a blockage in the Strait of Malacca caused by piracy, whereas geopolitics does. The international relations of Western Europe or Australia cannot really contend with the problem of territorial disputes in the South China Sea, whereas geopolitics can. Any change to the composition of the eurozone's membership may be an international relations issue for European nations, but it might well be considered geopolitics by investors from elsewhere in the world.

A Non-Quantifiable Risk

Geopolitics, however we choose to define it—and there are many ways to define it—is hard to quantify. Fund managers, by nature, often like to reduce reality to a number. In an era when algorithms govern investing and drive governance itself, it is easy to dismiss non-quantifiable risks. But it is dangerous to do so, as Daniel Yankelovich (1972), the father of modern polling, has written:

> The first step is to measure what can be easily measured. This is okay as far as it goes. The second step is to disregard that which cannot be measured, or give it an arbitrary quantitative value. This is artificial and misleading. The third step is to presume that what cannot be measured really is not very important. This is blindness. The fourth step is to say that what cannot be measured does not really exist. This is suicide.

Another aspect to consider is that geopolitics involves unknowns and is thus purely speculative and unworthy of time and attention. However, there is a difference between truly "unknown unknowns" and knowable or probable unknowns.[2] But fund managers will inevitably ask why they should bother at all if geopolitics cannot be quantified.

[2]As described in the famous briefing given by US Secretary of Defense Donald Rumsfeld on 12 February 2002 (www.defense.gov/transcripts/transcript.aspx?transcriptid=2636).

The modern "science" of economics has long tried to dissociate itself from the unquantifiable, using math as the wedge to distance itself from politics and its global counterpart, geopolitics. But as historian E.H. Carr (1939) rightly observed, "The science of economics presupposes a given political order and cannot be profitably studied in isolation from politics." Today, we could say that the *financial markets* presuppose a given political order and cannot be profitably studied in isolation from politics *or geopolitics*.

Because both politics and geopolitics are fluid, it is important to consider the following question: How much of my risk management (strategy, structures, institutions) assumes that politics and geopolitics will be stable? Fund managers build portfolios on a foundation of geopolitical assumptions. It is assumed that states will continue to exist when, in fact, coups, the establishment of military governments, and the dissolution of borders are ongoing possibilities. It is assumed that nations do not confiscate assets when, in fact, we see many examples of confiscations, from the Cypriot bank bailout in 2013 to the contests over territory in the South China Sea that involve "confiscations" of physical assets. It is assumed that conflict and war will not affect valuations, and yet the spillovers from the breakdown of stability in the Middle East raise the prospect of war, acts of terrorism, and the possibility of other market-moving events. It is assumed that borders are sound and reliable when, in fact, we see many borders being challenged or dissolved and incursions being made across them. The rise of "mapfare"—map warfare—is a telling example: nations challenging borders and territorial claims by issuing new maps of the geography in question.

What if the foundation on which asset management and investing are built resembles sand more than rock? What if geopolitics can touch the portfolio in a manner that could prove profitable or that should be guarded against?

Geopolitical risk can affect not only trading strategies but also the viability of the institutions that manage capital. Current examples include the Scottish referendum, which suddenly made a number of extremely large institutions and investors rethink whether their headquarters should stay in Scotland. Similarly, the Arab Spring rendered North Africa and much of the Middle East almost uninvestable for a time. But Dubai and Abu Dhabi, United Arab Emirates, have ended up serving as havens for regional capital. In less than a year after the Arab Spring began, Tunisia broke its own records for new and successful IPOs. The geopolitical tension between the United States, China, and Russia hardly existed a few years ago. Today, it has the potential to undermine the existing financial architecture and could lead to the creation of a new reserve currency that would replace the US dollar. These are all important, market-moving developments.

Geography and Politics

Geopolitics has always been closely tied to the act of mapping the world. The word *geopolitics* itself ties together geography and politics because geopolitics describes the efforts of states to project power beyond their own borders in the pursuit of their national interests.

Politics, in contrast, is "local," as Tip O'Neill, the late US Speaker of the House, famously put it. Most fund managers undoubtedly wish that politics and geopolitics would stay out of the markets and the world economy most of the time. But this view is rooted in several prejudices that overlook the simple fact that neither can be avoided. Both politics and geopolitics are central to the proper functioning of markets.

Markets depend on states to protect and defend property rights, contracts, and borders and to provide a judiciary and protection from opponents at home and abroad. In other words, the presence of a police force, a military force, and a judicial system has value to financial markets. If the state did not provide these protections, mob rule or organised crime or organised vigilantes would step in to fill the vacuum. States also play the essential role of raising government revenue so they can provide whatever civil society requires, including basic education, social safety nets, health care, and the like. But states are obliged to pursue their national interests, however those may be defined. Thus, states are required to project their influence abroad as well as manage other states' projections of power that touch their own citizens.

Benchmark Investing and Geopolitical Risk

Many fund managers may find themselves arguing that geopolitics does not matter to them because their investment decisions are benchmark driven. But even active managers who hug the benchmark have some latitude to alter the weightings around an index—and indeed must do so in order to justify their fees. These managers often find themselves engaging in what is called "agency risk." That is to say, they huddle together in the same views and trades because of the asymmetrical risk–reward relationship that is inherent in geopolitics.

A fund manager who tries to defy trends or make calls early will certainly be fired if good performance does not follow within a quarter or two at most. In contrast, a fund manager can survive immense losses so long as the entire industry or at least comparable competitors lose roughly the same amount for the same reasons. This "agency" problem further encourages the industry to turn a blind eye to the problem of geopolitics and renders the industry even more vulnerable to geopolitical events of which it is potentially unaware or for which it is ill prepared.

Black Swans

There is also a notable tendency, especially among business people and fund managers, to say that geopolitics is irrelevant because it is unpredictable by nature—it is a "black swan," as the philosopher and investment manager Nassim Taleb calls it in his book of the same name. It is likened to an act of God, an unpredictable event for which no fund manager or investor can be held accountable.

But the fact is that geopolitical events create both risks and opportunities. Investors and fund managers are accountable for leaving money on the table. Therefore, they cannot afford to assign arbitrary numerical weights to geopolitics or to be dismissive of, or blind to, the subject.

Prediction vs. Preparation

Luckily, however, investors and fund managers are smart people who understand what Richard Feynman, the renowned Nobel Prize–winning physicist, had to say about risk: "The first principle is that you must not fool yourself—and you are the easiest person to fool." No one can accurately predict what will happen on the geopolitical landscape. But as part of their fiduciary responsibility, fund managers can and should assess how much value is created by geopolitical stability or destroyed by geopolitical instability. This assessment can then underpin more-practical decisions about when risk can and should be taken or mitigated and when profits need to be pursued or protected.

The purpose of focusing on geopolitics is not to predict market- and price-moving events. Rather, it is to become more skilled at scanning the horizon and assessing scenarios so that investing strategies can become more robust when confronted by geopolitical developments.

In this primer, I sketch out ways to map risk, adding elements that complement the information that can be quantified and dealt with mathematically.

Investment and Geopolitics

Most books on geopolitics have been written by and for policymakers rather than by and for investors. These books tend to catalogue the geopolitics of the world, dividing the subject matter into local, regional, and national disputes, fault lines, philosophies, and security issues. Books on geopolitics often amount to historical timelines of events. Rather than doing that here, given what interests investors, it seems more practical to outline issues that can affect valuation, pricing, and risk management. Specific geopolitical events are perhaps better deployed as examples than as items to be catalogued.

The State as an Essential "Unit"

Sovereign or "country" risk has always been a central concern for investors. Obviously, every nation with borders constitutes an important investable "unit" or construct in the world economy. Financial indexes (e.g., the MSCI) and intergovernmental organisations (e.g., the World Bank, the IMF, the UN, and the World Trade Organization) all assume that states can be treated as discrete components. Geopolitics, as it relates to investors, begins with the assumption that the unit of membership is a "state" or "nation" with its own government and borders. These "sovereign" units called "states" or "nations" constitute the building blocks of investment strategy. Sovereign risk, therefore, is at the heart of investment strategy.

The Social Contract

Sovereign risk and dealings with "the state" are important matters even for purely domestic investors. After all, even the domestic investor has to ask questions about the nature of the relationship between a state and its citizens. Every state has a "social contract" with its citizens—the "deal" that always exists between citizens and their states. The terms of the deal differ widely, but in the main, citizens pay their taxes and agree to abide by the laws of citizenship in exchange for a set of promises the state offers. States are called upon to provide defense, internal law and order, some sort of reliable judiciary, and some kind of commitment to public services, including health care, education, and the like.

The terms of the social contract in France are bound to be markedly different from the terms in the United States or, say, North Korea. The state may compel its citizens to abide by the laws of citizenship, though history shows that such arrangements are less enduring, or the citizens may voluntarily choose to abide. Either way, sovereign risk arises when the citizens decide to change (to renegotiate) the social contract. This decision to renegotiate can be expressed in various ways. For example, it can be expressed by voting out a government at the ballot box or by violent revolution in the streets. Obviously, prices and markets are bound to be affected whenever such events occur. In the main, orderly changes are priced differently than disorderly changes. Fund managers spend a good deal of time trying to understand how actions or inactions by a sovereign will affect valuations and the landscape of risk and opportunity even if the context is purely domestic.

These days, most investors invest across borders. Therefore, domestic actions by nondomestic sovereigns can affect investors. Similarly, owners of real assets in eastern Ukraine might no longer be sure whether they own their assets or under whose jurisdiction their assets now fall. Once it became clear that a majority of Scottish voters might vote yes on the referendum to grant Scotland independence (as we now know, the noes carried the day), many investors deemed it necessary to move their assets into other areas of the United Kingdom. Investors in natural gas assets in the eastern Mediterranean might think their risk lies with Cyprus and Israel, given that Cyprus owns the territory and Israeli firms hold most of the development licenses. But these gas fields could become the subject of disputes because other countries—including Greece, Lebanon, Turkey, and Egypt—have started to lay claim to some of the gas fields. Geopolitical actions by any of these states could affect the valuations of these assets. Or consider the attacks on Chinese nationals that occurred in factories throughout Ho Chi Minh City in 2014. These attacks were in response to news headlines about China's efforts to harvest energy from interior waters that the Vietnamese perceive as their own. These are all geopolitical risks.

The Power to Tax

The state's power to tax is essential to its survival. No state can exist without some capacity to generate a budget and provide for its basic needs, which serves the interests of its citizens. Sovereign risk arises when a state seeks to take wealth or assets away from investors without their consent, whether or not those investors are its own citizens. It also arises when a sovereign cannot provide the basic necessities for investing: a legal system, law and order, a defense structure, and a social contract.

Even exclusively domestic asset managers and investors cannot ignore geopolitics. A purely "domestic" approach for dealing with sovereign risk is not viable for investors and fund managers partly because of the speed at which information travels and at which investment parameters can change. The interconnectedness of the world economy and global markets gives rise to substantial correlation risk. Changes in one part of the world can lead investors to sell or buy assets in otherwise unrelated locations. Correlation risk alone requires investors to factor in geopolitics even when dealing with purely domestic portfolios. The cheapness or costliness of capital in one part of the world can have a material impact on the relative cheapness or costliness of capital in another. A sovereign state may appear attractive or unattractive on its own, but global investors will always rank a nation relative to its peers.

A sovereign's "risk," or country risk, has always been closely linked to its financial position. Typically, a nation's balance sheet becomes "unbalanced" when the nation spends beyond its means. Throughout history, excessive debt has usually arisen from the expenses of warfare. Over the last 100 years, government debt, especially among the rich industrialised nations, has also come about as the result of overpromising benefits and public services. Sometimes the markets are amenable to such excessive spending and are willing to tolerate financial imbalances for prolonged periods. In other cases, even a small step in the direction of imbalance can be met with a sharp withdrawal of investor interest.

Either way, investors should pay close attention to a sovereign's financial situation because governments are inclined to use their power to tax to resolve cash constraints. The balance between the power of the state to tax and the power of an individual or a corporation to generate a profit lies at the heart of the social contract. States that overtax their citizens destroy the incentive to work. Examples include the former Soviet Union, which formally ceased to exist in 1991. One reason for its demise, among many possible explanations, is that it simply ran out of income sufficient to follow through on the promises it had made to its citizens.

Under Prime Minister Harold Wilson, Britain saw the tax rate rise to 83% on wage and salary incomes and to 98% on investment income—an event that culminated in significant social unrest (the "Winter of Discontent") and the need to ask the IMF for a bailout. A generation later, the Arab Spring resulted, at least in part, from the public's unwillingness to continue seeing most of the Arab nations' wealth channelled into the hands of a very small elite. The revolutionaries preferred a system in which wealth and taxes would be both generated and redistributed more evenly and fairly.

A state can raise money in many ways, some of which fall within the agreed-on social contract while others violate it. In either case, there can be consequences for investors who have to consider the risk of higher taxation or reduced delivery of expected public services. They must be alert to other, more aggressive forms of taxation, including expropriation, confiscation, and even inflation, which is a hidden tax that can be considered a stealthy form of confiscation.

Sovereign Risk and National Balance Sheets

The normal barometer of sovereign risk is the rate of interest at which investors are willing to lend capital to the sovereign. Normally, all other risk assets in an economy are priced against sovereign risk. In recent years, government spending beyond means has been so excessive—and sovereign debt has become so risky—that many governments have had to resort to highly unconventional monetary policies to sustain stability in the financial markets. These policies are generally known as *quantitative easing* (QE). This term encompasses components of or additions to QE, such as "forward guidance," whereby central banks commit not only to offer extremely low interest rates but also to give the markets substantial warning in advance of any change in monetary policy.

Currently, there are significant uncertainties about sovereigns, interest rates, and risk assessment because of the debt crisis and the policy response to it. Although governments may have avoided a catastrophe by engaging in QE and by pushing interest rates down, government debt problems cannot generally be "fixed" by adding more debt. Some even argue that US and G–7 government bonds, which used to represent the so-called risk-free rate of return, may now represent the "return-free rate of risk." If a pure cash flow metric is applied to sovereigns, it is not hard to make the case that some small African nations are more likely than many of the industrialised nations to pay back their debt in full and on time. Yet the risk models the markets rely on continue to assume that the United States and the G–7 are the least risky sovereigns—in spite of the unusual measures that have been taken to prop them up in light of their financial imbalances.

Sovereign Powers

Markets ascribe value to the fact that a sovereign has powers that other investable entities do not have. A sovereign can print money. It can tax and expropriate assets, if necessary. It can change the law. It can arrest or militarily confront its opponents, whether internal or external. It has many qualities and capabilities that encourage the markets to apply a different analysis to its balance sheets and attendant risk than would ever be used in the case of a private sector firm or an individual. Markets clearly ascribe a value to having these qualities and capabilities; therefore, any enhancement to or infringement of them changes the price of sovereign risk. In other words, geopolitics—through either its absence or its presence—has an undeniable impact on asset prices.

Quantitative Easing and Geopolitics

QE creates an ironic twist in the tale of modern geopolitics. In an effort to protect against sovereign risk, central banks have injected record sums of money into the world economy, thus driving down both volatility and the cost of insuring against risk while driving up asset prices. As a result, fund managers are disinclined to spend money on insurance of any kind (including the hedging of everyday risks, let alone insuring against unlikely risks). When both the price of money and the level of volatility fall, even as historic geopolitical events are unfolding, the industry is encouraged to believe that it does not have to pay any attention to such risks. Why bother when there are assurances that central banks will "fix" any problems caused by geopolitics—or anything else—by simply adding more liquidity?

Meanwhile, central banks have had to engage in QE precisely because governments are so deeply in debt that they are often incapable of sustaining military action or expenditures. In other words, QE reflects the fact that sovereign risk is so high that nations must engage in unconventional monetary policies to address the severity of the problem.

This inability or disinclination to respond arguably invites other states to test the boundaries of both territory and diplomacy, thus increasing the risk of geopolitical events.

Geopolitics as Mapping

And so, geopolitics comes back to geography and mapping. Rather than starting with a history of the definition of geopolitics, it might be more engaging for a fund manager or investor, whose attention is inevitably drawn to the future rather than the past, to begin with an image of the global map. Imagine a three-dimensional holograph of the world rather than a two-dimensional map. Or consider a cartogram, such as **Figure 1**—that method of mapping in which the size of each territory reflects a variable (e.g., population, natural resources, or government spending) rather than its actual geographic size. In this way, we can begin to plot out the realms in which geopolitics affects markets and prices. For example, there is a section later in this book about how modern warfare is conducted. Although it can be fought on the ground with boots and blood, modern technology permits its conduct in new locations, including cyberspace and outer space. Global markets now depend heavily on both for almost everything that matters to daily life: telecommunications, the Global Positioning System (GPS), and the World Wide Web.

Recent developments in computer technology mean that an opponent can be stopped or hindered more efficiently and less expensively by inserting a thumb drive that releases a disabling computer virus than by dropping a bunker buster. Similarly, computer technology has allowed geopolitics to creep into the daily concerns of financial and business institutions that are now constantly hacked into and spied on, not only by private attackers but also by states—friendly, unfriendly, domestic, and nondomestic alike—and by non-state actors that can fairly easily hijack a firm's data or systems to hold for ransom.

Figure 1. Cartogram of the Global Population

Source: Copyright www.worldmapper.org. Reprinted with permission.

Nuclear Weapons

Investors and fund managers have not had to think very much at all about nuclear weapons since the fall of the Soviet Union. For the most part, such instruments of power have been tightly controlled and contained under a web of carefully crafted nuclear nonproliferation treaties and policies. But these treaties are now weakening or being abandoned as the superpowers reassert their right to deploy nuclear weapons. China, Russia, and the United States all have or are testing hypersonic vehicles that can deliver a nuclear payload to almost anywhere in the world in less than an hour. In 2014, the United States formally accused Russia of violating the Intermediate-Range Nuclear Forces Treaty (INF Treaty) after Russia allegedly fired RS-24 ("Yars") and RS-26 ("Rubezh") ICBMs. Russia, China, and the United States have all moved nuclear weapons into closer proximity to their opponents in recent years.

Technology has moved on as well, allowing states to build and deliver powerful weapons that may not fall under traditional treaty terms. In addition, the speed of delivery has been vastly enhanced, and thus any return to an arms race will permit policymakers far less time to consider their responses to geopolitical events. The Cuban Missile Crisis may have seemed a high-pressure environment. But what took 10 days to address and resolve in 1962 might be compressed into minutes or hours today. Consider the speed of Russia's response to the possibility that Ukraine might join the EU, thus bringing NATO to Russia's doorstep in the south. From Russia's perspective, this episode was another Cuban Missile Crisis.

More and more small countries are seeking to acquire nuclear or sophisticated weapons capabilities. In the Middle East, for example, Saudi Arabia, Turkey, and Egypt have all announced their intention to obtain nuclear weapons, given that Israel arguably has such weapons and Iran may be trying to develop them. The superpowers and other nations increasingly fear one particular development that is at least as toxic to peace and stability—namely, a "dirty bomb" in the hands of a non-state actor.

Frankly, the weaponisation of small states and non-state actors is already apparent. That is how a non-state actor like Hezbollah was able to sink an Israeli ship in 2006. Hezbollah used a Chinese-made C-802 anti-ship missile that had not previously been known to be in the control of or used by a non-state entity. Similarly, if ethnic Russian separatists in Ukraine are capable of downing a commercial aircraft, regardless of who supplied them with the weapon, it is a warning that weapons have evolved in such a way that non-state groups can securely control and deploy them. One of the great geopolitical worries is that Pakistan becomes destabilised and nuclear material or weapons fall into the hands of the Taliban or some other non-state actor that would make ill use of them. But trouble can arise without such weapons. Conventional small arms have spread throughout the world. They may be enough to cause geopolitical pressures without any sophisticated technology.

Bioweapons

Recent developments in technology have forced investors to take leaps of imagination and to consider the idea that warfare can now be conducted at the subcellular and even subatomic level thanks to advancements in nanotechnology and biogenetics. Today's technology enables scientists to craft biological, DNA-based viruses that affect only one individual, thus forcing security and intelligence services around the world to both protect the DNA of their own leaders and gather the DNA and other markers of other countries' leaders.[3]

The idea of "warfare" has expanded dramatically in the post–World War II environment. No longer are physical weapons required. Information and knowledge can be a ready substitute for a battlefield. Industrial espionage, spying, and clandestine operations in general are now back on the landscape of the world economy in a way that has not been seen since Ian Fleming, John le Carré, and Tom Clancy wrote their spy novels about the Cold War. The public disclosure of the existence of America's Echelon, Prism, and "Five Eyes" programs and of the state-sponsored espionage capabilities of China, Russia, and others has brought into focus that the world has entered a new era of espionage risk. Today, the objective is not only to damage or destroy others' capabilities but also to read and hear their thoughts in order to outbid or outmaneuver them in the effort to acquire valuable assets.

[3]Andrew Hessel, Marc Goodman, and Steven Kotler, "Hacking the President's DNA," *Atlantic* (November 2012).

3. A History of the Word *Geopolitics*

Our holographic, or cartographic, view of the global landscape can be stripped down to reveal the origins of geopolitics. This exercise will show that the geopolitical issues investors face today may be occurring on a new plane, or in new dimensions, but the fundamental drivers are not so different from those in the past.

Politics vs. Geopolitics

Where is the dividing line between politics and geopolitics? Politics and policy are typically considered domestic in nature even if local politics has global causes or consequences. Geopolitics, in contrast, presumes political and policy decisions that have deliberate consequences beyond the domestic territory and population. Of course, the question of intent leaves the line between politics and geopolitics remarkably blurry.

An intent-based definition does not serve well in the modern world economy because it precludes a domestic policy that happens to have global consequences, such as a decision by the US Federal Reserve to change the level of interest rates. Inside the United States, this decision is clearly "policy," not "geopolitics." But outside the United States, such a policy decision could be considered to have immense global consequences that render it a "geopolitical" or "geo-economic" policy as far as observers are concerned. Similarly, a decision by China to weaken or strengthen its currency may seem to be domestic policy to the Chinese, but it certainly has global consequences with respect to the United States and other nations.

Some might prefer to reserve the term geopolitics for military matters alone, hoping to separate military power from political power. But in a world where economic policy can have even greater consequences than the use of military equipment, there must be some innovation in our thinking. After all, which would do more damage to an industrialised country like the United States, the United Kingdom, or Japan: attacking it with an army or simply selling the outstanding sovereign debt and pushing up interest rates by several percentage points?

Power and Sovereignty Are Indivisible

The Council on Foreign Relations and many others still try to distinguish between geo-economics and geopolitics, making the assumption that one involves commerce and the other involves the use of military might or purely political or policy tools. But if we look at the origins of geopolitics, it becomes clear that the instruments of state power and statecraft remain inseparable. The difficulty arises from the persistent belief that the two, economics and politics, can be disentangled. This belief, in part, causes strategic security experts to remain relatively ignorant of economics and causes economics experts to remain relatively ignorant of strategic security issues.

In contrast, politicians and policymakers are well aware of the vast array of tools and instruments they can wield to serve the national interest. How interesting that Joseph Chamberlain, the UK Secretary of State for the Colonies, said at a dinner in 1902, "You young gentlemen have entertained me royally, and in return I will give you a priceless secret. Tariffs! They are the politics of the future." We have moved on from tariffs for the most part, but economics as an objective and tool of statecraft remains in place.

One can try to refine the definition of geopolitics by exploring the terms geo-economics, geostrategic, and other such derivations, but in the end, geopolitics exists in reality even if it is not well dealt with by theory. As Carr (1939, pp. 119–120) said,

> Power is indivisible; and the military and economic weapons are merely different instruments of power . . . [and] in the pursuit of power, military and economic instruments will both be used.

Jean-Jacques Rousseau noted that sovereignty is itself indivisible. In his *Social Contract and Discourses*, he wrote, "Whenever Sovereignty seems to be divided, there is an illusion."[4] Nations are obviously obliged to pursue their national interests and use power in many forms to achieve their goals. They will make use of every tool available to them in the conduct of statecraft: political, economic, strategic, military, moral, and so on.

Geopolitics, therefore, is the practice of a sovereign's seeking to influence abroad, outside domestic territory, no matter which tool is used. The definition also encompasses the practice of a sovereign's defending against or managing efforts by other nations to project power and influence onto itself or its nationals. Geopolitics can be offensive or defensive.

The "Geo" in Geopolitics

Although the conduct of statecraft, international relations, diplomacy, and war has existed for thousands of years, the word "geopolitics" was not introduced until the 20th century. In fact, it seems that the use of the word did

[4]*Social Contract and Discourses* caused an uproar across Europe when it was first published, in 1762, and was on the Vatican's Index of Forbidden Books. Hugely influential, it has remained continually in print for more than 250 years.

not become truly commonplace until the 1960s, around the time that a moon landing became feasible and people began to fully comprehend how quickly a nuclear warhead could travel from one continent to another. That was the moment when a "geospatial" view—a view of the world from space—began to replace the more traditional approach, which had involved merely state-to-state "international relations." Before then, the use of the "geo" was meant to convey a marriage between geography and politics.

When exploring traditional references to geopolitics, it is clear that most of the forefathers of the notion never actually used the word. Instead, they referred to the phenomenon.

Classical Geopolitics

There are several broad eras of geopolitics. The subject can be considered to have begun in 1832, when Carl von Clausewitz, the great military historian, wrote that "war is a continuation of *politik* by other means." Although the quote is often translated using "policy" for *politik*, the German word *politik* combines "politics" and "policy" into one. Clausewitz thus began an alignment between the concept of politics and the projection of power beyond national borders.

The "classical" era of geopolitics focused on the practical elements of power projection. Several thinkers pursued the notion of "politics through geographical control." In 1890, Alfred Thayer Mahan argued that sea power was the key to success in his famous book *The Influence of Sea Power upon History, 1660–1783*. This tome was followed, in 1902, by H.J. Mackinder's book *Britain and the British Seas* and, in 1904, by his article "The Geographical Pivot of History." In that article, he established geography, and the conquering of it, as a principal focus of politics. In contrast to Mahan, Mackinder focused on land. He introduced the idea of a "Heartland." If one controlled that, one controlled the world. For him, the Heartland was a "pivot area" that encompassed Eastern Europe through Russia and into Asia.

At roughly the same time, in 1897, Friedrich Ratzel published *Politische Geographie*, which focused much more on the acquisition and exercise of power through control of land and space. He introduced the word *lebensraum* (living space), which was later picked up by his student Rudolf Kjellén, who was the first person to use the term geopolitics—in 1916, in the introduction to *Swedish Geography and the State as a Living Form*. Kjellén added the words *volk* (people or folk), *reich* (realm), and *raum* (room or space) to Ratzel's ideas, further justifying the case for a nation's expansion. He also broadened the definition of "national interest" to include economic well-being, which went substantially beyond the mere law-and-order aspect of state power.

Karl Haushofer, a German general and geographer, applied these ideas in the field, which inspired his student Rudolf Hess to build the case for the enlargement of Germany. Haushofer used the term *wehrgeopolitik* (war *politik*). These ideas were picked up by the National Socialists in Germany and used as the basis for the German military–led expansion that culminated in World War II; Hess became deputy führer under Hitler.

Cold War "Bloc" Geopolitics

Naturally, the term geopolitics became generally discredited because of this history. However, in 1942, the Austrian émigré Robert Strausz-Hupé wrote a book titled *Geopolitics: The Struggle for Space and Power*, which opened the door to a new notion of geopolitics. Strausz-Hupé argued that the nation-state was over and that "power blocs" would emerge in its place—and that is roughly what happened. In reaction to the Nazis' use of the term, the post–World War II philosophy was to avoid geopolitics altogether by creating a system that permitted nations to deepen their common interests and thereby avoid the need for conflict. Instead of being called geopolitics, the tensions between the two main post–World War II power blocs—the Soviet Union and the United States—were referred to as the "Cold War." All other geopolitical issues had a tendency to be subsumed under that larger confrontation.

Balance of Power

The European experience of war was that it was usually caused by the desire to acquire someone else's land and resources or by the loss of a "balance of power." This latter idea lies at the heart of the study of geopolitics. It assumes that nations are unlikely to challenge each other if their abilities to project power are roughly the same. Balance of power generally refers to weapons capabilities, or possibly manpower capabilities. It implies the ability to deter a potential opponent. The wars in Europe were typically driven by the absence of a balance of power, by the desire to acquire territory and commodities, and by the belief that increasing national power at the expense of another nation would be worthwhile (as outlined by Kjellén and others, described earlier).

Shortly before World War I, an idea emerged that has underpinned geopolitics ever since: the idea of world peace through world institutions. The hope was that a supranational entity could resolve disputes through arbitration, negotiation, and diplomacy; enforce the disarmament of nations; and resolve conflicts without any need for war. In 1910, this idea was promoted by Sir Norman Angell in his book *The Great Illusion*, in which he argued that peace could be achieved through economic interdependence and global institutions. He was awarded the Nobel Peace Prize for these ideas in 1933.

In practical terms, these ideas came to fruition in the form of the League of Nations, which was established in 1919. It did not work. World War II broke out a mere 20 years later. But this hopeful idea was expanded into the multitude of institutions we see today, including the United Nations and the World Trade Organization, among others.

The Origins of the EU: Geopolitics

During the interwar period, there was an intense debate about whether this supranational approach was flawed. Though designed to ensure that everyone benefitted and that no one would have reason to resort to war, it often produced uneven results. The immense burden of paying off war debts trapped nations in long periods of low growth and high unemployment, which in turn motivated some to fight for a better "deal." Access to commodities also remained a contentious issue. There are many arguments to be had over the causes of World War II, but it is clear that Germany and France ended up prepared to fight a war over who would own the steel-making resources in the area we now call Alsace-Lorraine, on the French–German border. The initial cornerstone of postwar European geopolitics was the European Coal and Steel Community (ECSC), created by the Treaty of Paris in 1951, which forced the two nations to share Alsace-Lorraine's coal and steel resources.

This core supranational concept was proposed by two Frenchmen: Robert Schuman (the French foreign minister) and Jean Monnet (who had served in the exiled French government during World War II). In his famous "Schuman Declaration" of 9 May 1950, Schuman declared:

> The pooling of coal and steel production should immediately provide for the setting up of common foundations for economic development as the first step in the federation of Europe and will change the destinies of those regions which have long been devoted to the manufacture of munitions of war, of which they have been the most constant victims.

Monnet laid the groundwork for this approach with his "Theory of l'Engrenage" (putting grit into the works), which proposed that war could be averted in future if the ability to forge weapons was denied to Germany. In practical terms, that meant giving political control over the Ruhr and Saar regions, where coal was mined and steel could easily be made, to France and giving commercial access to Germany. The ECSC evolved into the European Community and then the European Union. (Interestingly, Japan's entry into

World War II was encouraged, to some degree, by US efforts to cut off Japan's access to energy and steel-making supplies.)

At the core of the Bretton Woods system, however, was not the denial of access to raw materials but, rather, the idea that so long as goods and people could freely cross borders, there would be no need for military forces to do so. If enough wealth could be created from global trade, it would diminish the need for conflict. This is the central idea of the Bretton Woods system, which emphasised commitment to free trade and a US dollar–based trading system as a means of diminishing the risk of conflict—the origin of the "dollar bloc."

Two Blocs

So, Strausz-Hupé's notion of geopolitics' creating blocs did indeed come true. But in the aftermath of World War II, another bloc also emerged—the Communist bloc, as it was then called, which was dominated by the Soviet Union and characterised by its Communist philosophy. The dollar bloc, or Bretton Woods system, was dominated by the United States and characterised by its capitalist philosophy.

A balance of power between the two was believed to exist. The common economic interests within these blocs—and the balance of power that came from the nuclear and conventional weapons both sides had—managed to prevent conflict on a global scale. Of course, the two blocs were engaged in many local conflicts, from Vietnam to the Cuban Missile Crisis, but the prospect of a world war seemed to have subsided in the realm of geopolitics. Instead, the greatest worry was that the United States and the Soviet Union, in particular, might engage in nuclear conflict, which was a very different and more terrifying image of "world war."

Saul Cohen (2009, p. 24) has written that the "balance of power" (explained later in the book) between these two blocs "re-awakened" interest in geopolitics. But when conflicts began to unfold between the United States and the Soviet Union, all the events were simply subsumed under the term Cold War, even if geopolitics was indeed the subject at hand.

It was during this period that the views of Nicholas Spykman began to gain momentum. He became known as the "godfather of containment" and argued, in 1942, that Mackinder had been wrong. The "Heartland" was not the key to power projection. The "Rimland" was the place where power would need to be projected (see Dodds 2007, p. 37). By Rimland, Spykman meant the coastal areas of Europe and Asia. In this way, the rise of the Soviet Union could be "contained" or restrained. This view set the stage for the competition between the United States and the Soviet Union for influence in the

Rimland, which included Vietnam (and the rest of Indochina), East Africa, India, and the Middle East.

In 1954, President Eisenhower confirmed that the United States and Communist powers were vying for control of the Rimland (specifically, Indochina) by announcing the "domino theory." He said that the "falling domino" principle meant that

> you have a row of dominoes set up, you knock over the first one, the second, and so on until all are knocked over. So, you could have a beginning of a world where either capitalists or communists successfully project power and gain influence over specific geographies, which would have profound consequences.[5]

This concept set the stage for US Secretary of State Henry Kissinger, who was also a national security adviser to the president, to use the term geopolitics from the mid-1960s until the late 1970s as he conducted the standoff with the Soviet Union in the Rimland. But Kissinger's use of the term has been criticised. The famed military historian Michael Howard (1994) wrote, "For Kissinger 'geopolitics' is simply a euphemism for power relationships. . . . [The] 'power politics' [Kissinger describes] is a concept (though not a practice) and what he was really talking about was 'the politics of power.'"

"New Geopolitics" of Globalisation

In 1989, any debate about geopolitics became moot with the demise of the Soviet Union. This event further reduced the need for the term because all "geopolitics" disappeared when that superpower ceased to exist. The United States emerged as the sole serious superpower. And most talk of "geo," or what goes on beyond one's own borders, was no longer focused on the possibility of conflict between nations but, rather, on the necessity of commerce and trade. Francis Fukuyama (1989) summed up the US view at the time: The Cold War had ended. The United States had "won" the intellectual argument between capitalism and Communism, and there was no longer any competition between superpowers. Only one superpower existed: the United States. Obviously (at least from the US point of view), geopolitics was over.

Globalisation became the catchword of the day because a more globally integrated world economy was assumed to work in the best interests of all the participants. Indeed, there was a keenness to find a new term to signify the new focus on the economic aspects of geopolitics.

At the time, John Agnew and Stuart Corbridge (1989) used the term "new geopolitics" in their essay "The New Geopolitics: The Dynamics of

[5]Press conference (7 April 1954).

Geopolitical Disorder": "It refers to the changing nature of the competition in the international arena, from the military-political sphere to the economic one." The historian and military strategist Edward Luttwak (1990) used the term "geo-economics" to emphasise that the competition was no longer for territory but for economic prosperity. Writing about this new economic focus, he described geo-economics as "the admixture of the logic of conflict and the methods of commerce." The simple idea was that growth rates and geopolitical power were interconnected and correlated.

The idea caught on, and President Clinton summed it up beautifully (albeit in a slightly different context) in his famous phrase, "It's the economy, stupid." His secretary of state, Warren Christopher, translated this campaign slogan into the realm of geopolitics in 1993, when he said, "In the post–Cold War world, our national security is inseparable from our economic security";[6] "the new centrality of economic policy in our foreign policy" is that "economic security is the foremost priority, ahead of the fate of the former Soviet Union or nuclear proliferation."[7]

After a decade of US efforts to persuade most countries to go in a capitalist direction, the geographer Saul Cohen (2009) concluded that the United States—and indeed the world—could never fully end or even contain geopolitics. Geo-economics might be a real phenomenon, but geography was still the key. In addition to the Heartland and the Rimland, Cohen focused on what he called the "Shatterbelts" (e.g., the Middle East and Africa), which were so fragile as to be unconvertible to capitalism and unmanageable in an era of globalisation. The military historian Robert Kaplan picked up on this idea that the geopolitics of certain parts of the world, such as Africa, was beyond management. For him, the North–South divide could not be surmounted. In 2012, he released his latest book, *The Revenge of Geography: What the Map Tells Us about Coming Conflicts and the Battle against Fate*, in which he returns to the idea that geography is the defining driver of geopolitics.

Zbigniew Brzezinski, who served as secretary of state under President Carter, also went back to the notion of geopolitics as geography in his book *The Grand Chessboard*, which came out in 1997. He talked about the need for the United States to control certain parts of the world in order to maintain its influence or at least deprive other potential superpowers of certain parts of the map. But even this former secretary of state did not feel comfortable with the term geopolitics and gave his book the subtitle *American Primacy and Its*

[6]Patrick Radden Keefe, *Chatter: Dispatches from the Secret World of Global Eavesdropping* (New York: Random House, 2005): 192.

[7]US Senate Foreign Relations Committee (4 November 1993); Warren Strobel, "Christopher Looks beyond the Recent Struggles at State," *Washington Times* (12 November 1993): A1.

Geostrategic Imperatives. He took Cohen's idea of Shatterbelts and extended it to a "global Balkans" concept whereby ancient and tribal disputes interrupt or interfere with global stability.

The one idea that persists throughout the modern use of the term geopolitics is that the superpowers will and must continue to project power internationally. Nature abhors a vacuum. Decisions to withdraw from geopolitics can create more geopolitics. The United States, Europe, China, and Russia might like to believe that they can avoid engaging with certain parts of the world without consequences. But the reality seems to be that absence from the global stage of geopolitics invites conflict just as much as presence does.

Paul Kennedy became the modern father of what is called "critical geopolitics," another post–Cold War notion of geopolitics, with his idea that such vacuums can be created by having insufficient funds to engage with the world. In his 1987 book, *The Rise and Fall of the Great Powers: Economic Change and Military Conflict from 1500 to 2000*, he suggested that a declining economy would mean increased (defensive) geopolitics, decreased influence, and less power projection, sooner or later. In other words, low economic well-being would put an otherwise powerful nation on the geopolitical defensive.

Meta-Geopolitics

There are other angles to geopolitics that one can explore. For example, Nayef Al-Rodhan (2012), the polymathic Oxford University professor, has written a book about *meta*-geopolitics in which he talks about the geopolitics of outer space and the competition for control of geostationary orbits and the like. Although this notion may sound fanciful at first, nations are fiercely competing for control of space these days. The ability to control or dominate space is a principal aim of national interest for the United States, China, Russia, India, and Japan. Smaller nations are also vying for corners of space. Society today depends heavily on space-based technology for satellite guidance systems, GPS, and other communications. Nearly all military equipment—certainly nuclear weapons—depends on physical assets in space. A common complaint in recent years is that some nations will blow up their own satellites just to create dangerous debris in orbits where other nations' space assets reside. There are also somewhat more mundane examples of reliance. Increasingly, farmers use satellites to resurface their land and achieve greater efficiencies with their use of water, chemicals, fertiliser, and seeds. Even Google has launched balloons into low-space altitudes as a means of delivering Wi-Fi connectivity to remote parts of the world. Clearly, outer space is a contested commercial and geopolitical arena.

Whose Geopolitics?

It would also be interesting to outline how Russia, China, India, and smaller nations have viewed geopolitics from their distinct perspectives, though, oddly, no such comprehensive reader or reference work seems to exist.

So, to repeat, geopolitics *generally* refers to a state's projection of power abroad by any means or tools of statecraft. This definition encompasses both the active effort to engage in geopolitics in order to project power externally and the passive effort to respond to the geopolitical efforts of others to project power. It encompasses all aspects of sovereignty and power, regardless of whether the tool or the objective is economic or political. The word "generally" is important because it leaves the door open to external non-state actors that increasingly are both the source of geopolitical pressures on states and the object of geopolitical efforts by states.

This definition still leaves many questions unanswered, such as which style of geopolitics is more effective—one driven by a utopian vision or a *realpolitik* approach? Does it matter to markets whether geopolitics is being pursued or managed by a democracy or by a capitalist autocracy? This question is especially important given that investors have tended to find autocracies like China easier to invest in than democracies like India. Government control increases certainty, to a degree. And yet, the greater the autocratic nature of the government, the more difficult it is for innovation to flourish because of the constraints on personal freedom. Fund managers struggle with their desire for the certainty that autocracy brings and the loss of freedom that it implies. Similarly, they struggle with their desire for the freedom to innovate that democracy offers and the uncertainty that is inherent in balancing competing interests.

But the critical issue for fund managers and investors remains: How can an investor understand the relationship between geopolitics and valuation? Investors need to think about the value that markets ascribe to the presence or absence of geopolitical concerns.

4. Weighing and Measuring

Practitioners in the field of geopolitics use a few key measures when analysing country and geopolitical risk that may be useful for fund managers and investors to consider. For example, borders tend to be artificial, manmade constructs that are subject to debate and change over time. This fact matters given that borders define an investment unit called a state. Border disputes can become important for purposes of valuation and pricing. Many border disputes are potentially relevant to markets.

Some border disputes attract ongoing attention. China and most of its neighbors are engaged in major disputes about who owns what in the South China Sea. The arguments are pursued through "mapfare"—that is, each nation puts out its own maps of the territory with its own claims to specific areas. For example, China's "10-dash line map," which (among other things) seems to incorporate Taiwan, contrasts with the maps issued by the Philippines and other Pacific nations. Japan and Russia continue to dispute the Kurile Islands, which each country includes on its own maps. Increased physical presence in a disputed territory, whether by military or commercial ventures, is another way to claim an area.

Incursions across borders are important signals for markets. Air and land incursions that test border responses have been increasingly common in recent years. Whereas market investors tend to downplay or ignore these events as noise, states are compelled to protect or pursue their national interests, ensuring that such events are always met with a response.

Effective National Territory

One useful measure, then, is to compare national borders with *effective national territory* (ENT). Developed by geographer David Hooson (1966, p. 342), the central idea of ENT is that it represents "a major part of the country which consistently produces a surplus in relation to its population and which, by implication, is therefore supporting the country in a very real sense." The needs and interests of one part of a nation can be an important driver of national interest in general.

One can think of several pertinent examples: Australia is divided between the west, which produces wealth from mining, and the east, which contains most of the population. This uneven distribution of raw-material wealth and demographics creates interesting, market-relevant tensions. Australia's defense strategy is tied to that of the United States, but the economy, especially in the west, is tied to China's economy. As the United States and China spar over territorial and other issues, that tension creates important geopolitical pressures for Australia that require attention and management.

Ecumenes

Another important geopolitical feature is the *ecumene*. An ecumene is a core geographical area, one with special significance. Cohen (2009, p. 35) uses the term to refer to areas with the greatest population density and the greatest density of wealth creation: "The most advanced portion of the state economically, it is usually its most important political area." In most countries, stress always exists between political/economic centres and other regions. For example, in the United Kingdom, there is an ongoing argument about the relative power of London versus the rest of the United Kingdom. London generates at least 20% of the tax revenue for the nation and substantially more than its proportionate share of GDP. It is one of the fastest-growing and largest megacities in the industrialised world. But it has little autonomy from the central government in Westminster. Increasingly, it seeks to raise its own taxes and finance its own infrastructure. London has been approached by political leaders and investors from China, the sovereign wealth fund (SWF) of Norway, and other nations about investment deals in property and infrastructure that would strengthen London's ability to argue for more financial independence and greater freedom to generate its own tax revenue.

As another example of an ecumene that is relevant to investors, consider the situation in Nigeria. That nation has immense oil wealth. It is one of the largest suppliers of oil to the United States. Yet the southern part of Nigeria is wealthier than the northern part, where the oil actually comes from. The perceived inequality in the distribution of oil wealth stimulates all kinds of political and geopolitical pressures, from separatist movements to terrorist attacks. Any disruption to Nigeria's oil supply to the West caused by these forces would be considered a geopolitical event by investors.

Arguably, the world itself has certain ecumenes that matter to investors. If we think about the possibility of disruptions to major choke points in the world economy, we are forced to consider geopolitics. For example, ISIL in Iraq has threatened to disrupt tanker traffic in the Suez Canal. Such an event would certainly be considered geopolitical. China's fear of US power over the Panama Canal has led it to finance the construction of a new canal in Nicaragua, which would provide an alternate route between the Pacific and the Atlantic Oceans. China's presence in Latin America and its control of an alternate route could be perceived as a strategic threat to the United States.

The new canal would stimulate commerce between Latin America and China (and the rest of Asia) and thus attract investment. Once again, geopolitics bears down on market activities.

Extra-Territorial Allegiances

A state might have allegiances from people living outside its *national* borders. Cultural, tribal, and historical affiliations sometimes mean that a border does not coincide with a group of citizens who want to pledge their allegiance to a state they do not live in. The Middle East is rife with such examples. Recently, the actions of pro-Russian separatists along Russia's borders have raised renewed awareness that borders and territorial integrity can break down. Some might argue that President Putin's use of the word *Novorossiya* (New Russia) suggests that Russia might want to return to its imperial borders or at least welcome the various pro-Russian separatists who live beyond Russia's borders back inside them.

As another example, it could be argued that Mexico, or at least the area along the US border, is increasingly fluid and lacking in territorial integrity. Some would argue that the border is effectively moving north as migration pushes in from Mexico. Others might argue that the border is moving south, driven by increased investment and integration between the United States and Mexico and rendering Mexico part of the effective national territory of the United States.

The degree of affiliation and alignment may vary substantially. The French colonists in North Africa felt themselves to be part of France. The Irish diaspora also felt an alignment with their home country, but they did not seek to push their state of residence toward either a breakup or a different alignment with Ireland.

One way for investors to think about geopolitical risk is to consider not only current borders but also the possibility that borders might be "mean reverting," as we say in the markets.

Non-Effective National Territory

ENT is mirrored by *non-effective national territory* (N-ENT). There are places on the planet that are effectively ungoverned and potentially ungovernable owing to their remoteness or to a lack of interest on the part of the sovereign. The eastern arm of India—including Arunchal Pradesh, especially along the border with Bhutan—has long been considered a "not very effective" national territory of India. Similarly, Thailand finds it hard to manage or police its border with Myanmar (Burma), an area renowned for drug trafficking.

Many countries claim various rock formations in the South China Sea as their own but cannot effectively police or protect them from challenges by other countries. The US foothold in Diego Garcia in the Indian Ocean is of great strategic importance to the United States even though it is not part of US territory. Kaliningrad is ENT for Russia. Although owned outright by Russia, Kaliningrad is not necessarily as easy for Russia to govern as its mainland territory. Mutual weapons-inspection treaties and limited airspace force Russia to cooperate with Kaliningrad's neighbors to a greater extent than might occur in other parts of Russia.

Non-effective national territory is becoming a significant issue in geopolitics again. Places that are effectively without administration or that the sovereign cannot control even though physically inside its legal borders are magnets for geopolitical pressures and events. A few examples follow.

As mentioned previously, India's Arunchal Pradesh and its Himalayan borders are remote and thus quite hard to govern effectively. The Falkland Islands are again being claimed by Argentina. In 2014, announcing the issuance of a new bank note, the president of Argentina declared:

> This is a[n] homage to our Islas Malvinas and to all those who gave their lives to this cause. It will compel every Argentinian to keep alive on a daily basis the flames of love for our islands which are and always will be Argentinian.

The weakness of the Argentine economy, damaged by inflation and slow growth, has increased the need to generate revenue. The Falkland Islands have immense natural resources in the form of protein (fish and sheep) and, arguably, energy (natural gas and oil) now that technology has improved the capability to extract energy resources in difficult locations and more cost effectively. Perhaps unsurprisingly, Argentina occasionally tests whether the Falklands constitute effective or non-effective national territory of the United Kingdom. Is it an area the United Kingdom would still be prepared to protect and defend?

If that sounds far-fetched, think about the efforts of Spain to test British resolve regarding Gibraltar. In 2013, Britain and Spain sparred over fishing rights off Gibraltar. Spain has long claimed ownership of Gibraltar. In the end, the British sent a warship (a frigate), the HMS *Westminster*, to Gibraltar as a show of force, which quelled the dispute.

N-ENT need not be merely a physical location. It can also apply to a situation in which the economy or market function begins to be controlled by unwelcome non-state actors. The rise of organised crime in Greece might be one example. In the aftermath of the financial crisis, the various defaults (or haircuts), and increased austerity, the ability of organised crime to get a foothold has grown. Statistics show that organised crime activity has been steadily rising in Greece. The alignment of such opposition groups as the right-wing Golden Dawn Party with organised crime culminated in the arrest of the party's leadership and of several military officers accused of fomenting a coup.

Surely, a military coup, backed by organised crime, in a eurozone nation would qualify as a bona fide geopolitical event. The fact that the government alleges that this coup was attempted means that investors cannot afford to ignore the possibility of such seemingly implausible events. It shows that any nation that finds its effective control over its own territory reduced will necessarily have higher geopolitical risk factors.

Commodity Strength and Commodity Vulnerability

One final measure of geopolitical risk arises from dependence on commodities. Some states are blessed with access to valuable resources. Saudi Arabia has oil. The United States has natural gas. Greenland has rare-earth metals. The Himalayas have water. National interest and foreign policy are heavily defined by a nation's degree of access to natural resources. China's foreign policy and national interest are strongly motivated by its relative lack of water and domestically grown food, as the cartogram in **Figure 2** vividly illustrates. Russia's foreign policy and national interest are substantially driven by the fact that Russia supplies energy to Western Europe. And in return, Western Europe's policy stance strongly reflects its energy dependence on Russia.

Figure 2 reveals that countries with adequate supplies of water are greatly outweighed by those populous nations experiencing water insecurity.

Commodities are a traditional source of conflict among states. This fact still drives geopolitics today. Otherwise, banning food imports and prohibiting, for national security reasons, foreign entities from investing in domestic "critical assets" would be non-issues.

Shipping Lanes

Investors tend to think too narrowly about commodities. They assume that this topic is limited to oil and gas, iron ore and steel, water, wheat, livestock, and a few other basic materials. But other commodities also have geopolitical importance. Shipping lanes, for example, are a precious commodity, given that some 80% of global trade traverses the high seas. Although many nations claim that they seek to protect shipping lanes from disruption, not all would agree. For example, the United States says it is there to protect the shipping lanes for the benefit of all, including China. However, the

Figure 2. Cartogram of Global Water Insecurity

Source: Copyright www.worldmapper.org. Reprinted with permission.

suspicion in China is that the United States is trying to protect the shipping lanes *from* China, not *for* China. Similarly, China may say it shares this common interest, but the United States and its regional allies fear that China seeks to challenge the US presence on the high seas—as well as in space and cyberspace—as a means of serving China's national interests alone and not those of the broader community.

Price Stability

Price stability is a type of commodity. Any efforts to destabilise prices in the world economy usually translate into geopolitical events. Even a country like Zimbabwe, which has debased its currency more severely than any other nation so far this century, has managed to create a geopolitical risk issue for its neighbors. Others could argue that it has given a foothold in Africa to such outside parties as China. The expropriations of land and other privately held assets in Zimbabwe have arguably increased the taste for pursing expropriations elsewhere in Africa.

Raw Materials

The Arctic has become the centre of a formidable effort by many nations to lay claim to valuable strategic assets. The competition for a presence in the Arctic is aimed partly at ownership of strategic materials. President Putin is on record as saying that he expected some 20% to 25% of Russia's GDP to come from the incredibly rich Arctic resources, including oil, gas, minerals, gold, nickel, and even diamonds. Russia subsequently established a new division of its Federal Security Service, which deploys Special Forces commandos who are specifically trained for Arctic fighting. Other nations—including Norway, Canada, and even the United States—have moved more of their military command and control centres to the Far North in order to manage the potential threat to the integrity of their own territories. China currently has the fastest icebreakers and dominates the business of passing through Arctic waters. China has also strengthened its ties with Greenland, partly because of new finds of rare-earth metals there and partly because managing an Arctic strategy is easier with local physical access.

But some raw materials can also be acquired in purely commercial ways. Abu Dhabi's investment authority has honed its commodity-trading expertise in the hope that doing so will permit it to engage in purchases and M&A deals in the food industry, a move that will help cushion Abu Dhabi against food price fluctuations. China has emerged as an important buyer of US agribusiness and farm assets—its diminishing water supplies and huge population have raised the spectre of its being unable to feed itself, as depicted in **Figure 3** and **Figure 4**. The largest acquisition to date is the Smithfield deal, in which Shuanghui, a Chinese company, acquired the large US pork producer. In this way, China acquired not only a supply of pork but also access to the technology needed to render its own pork farmers more efficient.

Physical Footholds

In the aftermath of the financial crisis in Europe, China's state-owned entities were quick to realise that many assets would be for sale. In Greece, Chinese entities purchased the main port in Athens, at Piraeus, and apparently many agricultural assets as well. In Portugal, the Chinese found a number of available assets at good prices, including the possibility of building a forward base in the Azores. Neither the United States nor the European Union had the money to pay the rent on the old NATO airbase there; China has increasingly expressed an interest in paying a good price for the asset. Obviously, such an event would have significant geopolitical consequences.

The United States maintains physical footholds in many diverse locations, from Cuba (Guantánamo) to Diego Garcia in the Indian Ocean to a string of military bases in the Middle East and East Africa.

China has reinforced its foothold in the South China Sea by declaring an "air defense identification zone" across Chinese waters. This move requires non-Chinese, noncommercial aircraft to comply with China's demands.

India has recently announced its intention to enhance its physical and military infrastructure so that it can reach its Himalayan borders much faster. India worries about China's growing presence on the other side of the border. Investors should note that both sides accuse each other of border incursions.

Investors can consider many ways to measure geopolitical events and trends. But weighing their importance is a different task that cannot be so easily quantified.

Figure 3. Cartogram of Global Croplands

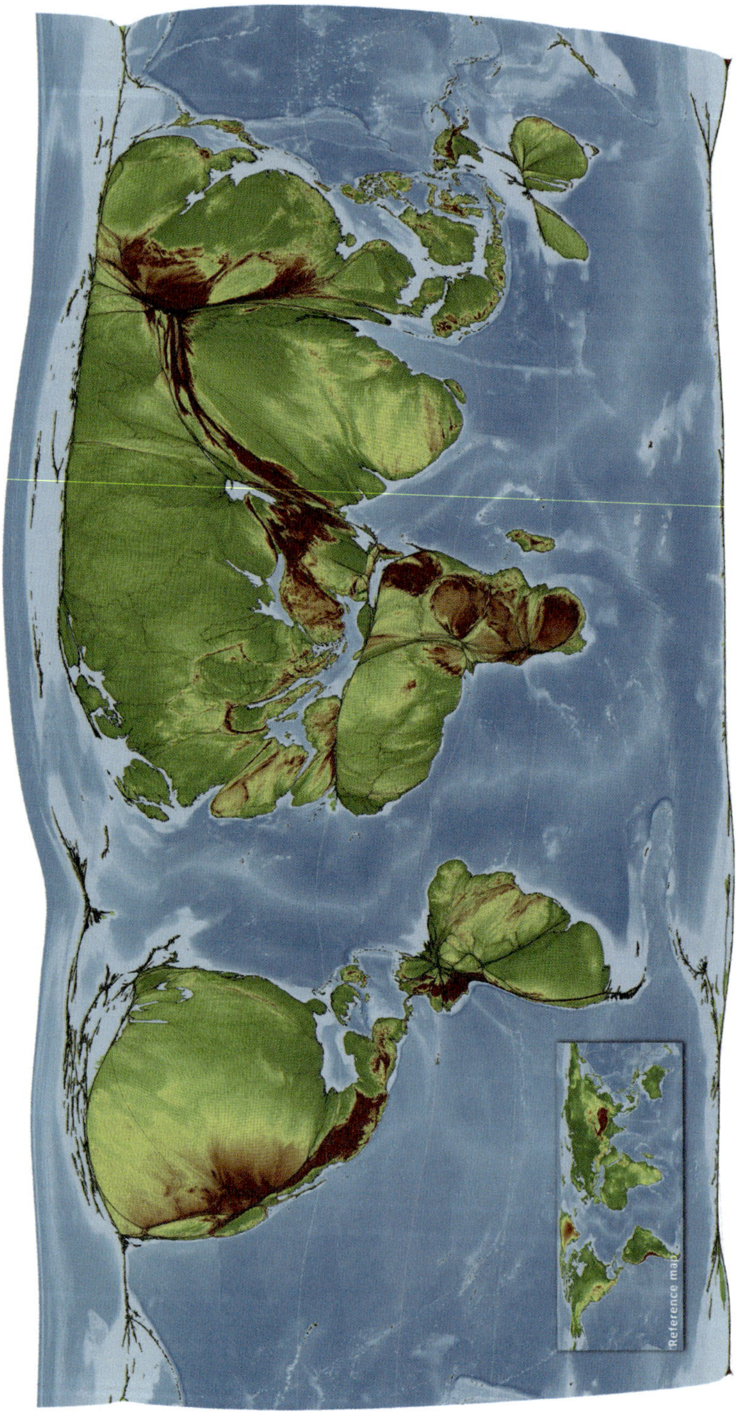

Source: Copyright www.worldmapper.org. Reprinted with permission.

Figure 4. Cartogram of Global Pastures

Source: Copyright www.worldmapper.org. Reprinted with permission.

5. World Order

It is often said that one of the greatest drivers of the prosperity of the 1990s and the following decade—until the 2007–09 financial crisis—was the rise of the "peace dividend." All the money spent on nuclear and other weapons, as well as the spending on troop deployments and materiel around the world—by the United States and Europe, but also by Russia and others during the Cold War—had been fundamentally unproductive. Although one could argue that weapons production generates GDP and employs workers, there is little doubt that it is much more productive to take the same talent, assets, and capital and redeploy them in the civilian economy, where they can pursue whatever innovations the economy is prepared to reward. Moreover, conflict is costly. Spending on conflict—even spending on its prevention—comes at a price.

Markets, therefore, ascribe some kind of value to geopolitical order and certainty. It is hard to decide how prices should move in response to geopolitical events if you have no idea how to ascribe value to peace or to conflict. Such extremes are not even necessary. The question is, What kind of world order increases or decreases market value?

What Is the World Order and How Much Is It Worth?

In 2014, Henry Kissinger published a book called *World Order*, in which he said, "The concept of order that has underpinned the modern era is in crisis." But what was the concept that underpinned the modern era? It is important to ask, because every generation—indeed, people from different countries and different philosophies—defines "world order" differently.

Some may not even know they hold a notion of a world order in their minds, but they do. For my father's generation (now in its 70s and 80s), there is typically a longing for the Bretton Woods era, when currencies were tied to the gold standard and almost everyone, except the Communists, believed that free markets were the fairest and most efficient way to build and distribute wealth in the world economy. Today, the notion of a gold standard is dismissed by policymakers, and by much of the public, as an extremist idea and a throwback, one that reveals a lack of understanding about modern finance.

Similarly, today's investors are likely to assume that the post–Berlin Wall world is "normal." They assume that there is an endless stream of emerging-market workers who are prepared to continuously push down wages and prices, thus eliminating the risk of inflation. They assume that growth rates are generally high because that is what happened, in most places, following the fall of the Berlin Wall. In such an environment, it makes much more sense to focus on getting rich than to focus on obtaining power. There is a tendency to continue assuming that the world order discourages conflict and encourages growth when, in fact, the circumstances that gave us the peace dividend have changed. Now that emerging-market workers are demanding higher wages and pushing prices up, the dynamics have changed. These workers are no longer sure they will be rich before they are old and are now more prepared to fight for political power instead of turning their energies to wealth generation alone.

Professional fund managers of the current generation, as well as most serious investors, are under the age of 50, which means they were born in or after 1964. The Strategic Arms Limitation Talks began in 1991, when members of this group were 27 or younger. So, they have grown up in a period when the peace dividend has allowed them to work in the world economy without having to focus on geopolitics very much. Of course, there have been geopolitical conflicts—some ongoing—since 1967. But from an investment perspective, these conflicts have, in the main, been regional and not global, so they have not affected global valuations. They have affected the investment landscape only in specific locations, which is why the market places higher valuations on industrialised countries that have relatively little conflict and lower valuations on those that have such a risk. The United States is traditionally viewed as a country with low geopolitical risk and Lebanon as one with high geopolitical risk, which is why the market has priced Lebanese assets much more cheaply than US assets.

In an ideal world, we could rely on a calm and peaceful investment environment. But geopolitical events can intrude on, damage, or destroy whatever benefits peace can bring. As R.G. Hawtrey (1930) noted, "If war is an interruption between two periods of peace, it is equally true that peace is an interval between two wars."

As is always the case, the current generation of fund managers and investors has been deeply influenced by its own experience. Thus, most have come to assume that world order rests on the relatively free movement of goods, people, and capital, underpinned by the idea that markets, rather than states or their governments, should determine the distribution of wealth and assets.

Competing Visions of World Order

There are many ways to think about the concept of world order. It is important to understand that colleagues, commercial adversaries, and allies alike may have very different visions of world order. Some see the current institutions (the Pax Americana, the Washington Consensus, the post–Bretton Woods system—there are many names) and principles as inherently biased.

Wallerstein's World Order. Another lens for viewing the world order comes from the political theorist Immanuel Wallerstein, who wrote the first volume of his series *The Modern World-System* in 1974. At the heart of his argument is the idea that political power is not as important as economic power. For Wallerstein, the degree of economic trade and interconnection between states defines hierarchy in the world order. His is a Marxist view of the world, but there is no doubt that many still see the world as a system in which a major country like the United States can systematically take advantage of smaller, less-developed nations.

The Clash of Civilisations. One may try to establish a world order, but it always remains vulnerable to what the political scientist Samuel Huntington called "the clash of civilizations," the title of his famous 1993 article in *Foreign Affairs*. Huntington refuted the idea that Francis Fukuyama had put forward (Fukuyama was his student), noting that we were not experiencing "the end of history." In fact, he said, there is a permanent "clash" driven by ancient ethnic and tribal rivalries that will always reappear in a contest for pure power regardless of how much wealth is created or how evenly it might be distributed. The conflicting interests of the various participants are so great—culturally, politically, and economically—that they cannot be reconciled except for relatively short periods. A given world order may exist, but it is constantly threatened by this "clash of civilizations." A modern example might be the efforts of the United States and other Western nations to introduce representative democracy in Iraq. Instead of democracy flourishing, Iraq has been declared a caliphate by a non-state actor.

In contrast, many dictatorships in the Middle East have been overthrown, making way for more-representative democracy. Tunisia is a good example. So, the bias is not one way only. The direction a culture clash takes is not predetermined.

Investors need to consider the risks to the portfolio or to the strategy that would arise from culture clashes. There are many examples. Ukraine has been a favoured location for agribusiness investment, given the richness of its soil and the fact that it is roughly the fourth-largest producer of food in the world. Some of these investments have become difficult to manage now that local separatists have broken away from the central government. These Russian-speaking separatists can be said to be involved in a culture clash with the local Ukrainian political leaders, whom they accuse of being "fascists." The two groups opposed each other during World War II and, arguably, even before the Russian Revolution, in 1918. In 1939, Leon Trotsky wrote:

> The Ukrainian question, which many governments and many "socialists" and even "communists" have tried to forget or to relegate to the deep strongbox of history, has once again been placed on the order of the day and this time with redoubled force.[8]

These cultural rivalries continue today, and as a result, the values of farmland and agribusiness investments in Ukraine have fallen substantially.

Culture clashes arise when a cultural group identifies more with its members than with the state it belongs to. Catalonia's efforts to separate from Spain are rooted in a culture clash. But generally speaking, the term is reserved for the deep religious and ethnic divides that seem to provoke ongoing conflicts throughout history.

Hegemons, Capitalist Democracies, and Autocracies

Any study of geopolitics must consider the various configurations of a world order.

One idea is that there must always be a *hegemon*, a single player that dominates the rest and can make and enforce the rules of the world order. The term is used in the sense that Britain was a hegemon during its imperial era, defining and enforcing its definition of world order. The United States has been the hegemon behind the post–World War II world order. Many believe that China has emerged as a regional hegemon.

Clearly, though, there have been long periods in history when there was more than one great power. The postwar period of competition between the United States and the Soviet Union thus led to the use of other definitions of world order, including a "bi-polar" and a "multi-polar" world order.

For an investor, the relevant question may have more to do with the character of the hegemon than with the fact that a hegemon exists. The values, principles, ethics, and ideals of a hegemon are bound to dominate the investment landscape. Investors are faced with the question in a different, more subtle way. A nation may be a liberal democracy, like the United States. Singapore stands as the best example of a capitalist autocracy—such governments are highly centralised, not welcoming of political challenges or internal conflict, prepared to quash opposition, and yet supportive of capitalist markets. In a capitalist autocracy, economic freedom is strongly promoted even as political freedom is strongly curtailed. China is now considered a capitalist autocracy even though it has a strongly Communist system of government. Russia is considered autocratic in a different sense. It has strong centralised control and economic freedom within limits.

---

[8]See www.marxists.org/archive/trotsky/1939/04/ukraine.html.

Perhaps the central geopolitical question facing this generation of investors relates to these extremes. Should investors favour liberal democracies, where investment decisions are subject to democratic political processes? Or is it more attractive to place capital with nations that take a more centralised and directive approach, curtailing individual freedoms in exchange for law and order? Is one philosophy better for innovation than the other? Is one better for capital generation or preservation?

States also have very different characteristics, characters, and qualities that influence the geopolitics they project and the way in which they manage others' projections. It is a wide-open debate whether democracies or capitalist autocracies are better for markets. The latter is a somewhat new form of government.

Democracies have long been considered the friendliest environment for commerce because personal political freedom aligns with personal economic freedom. But markets have tended to reward China, the capitalist autocracy, more than India, the democracy. Democracies are more difficult to predict. They find it harder to build infrastructure, and populist movements sometimes impose unexpected taxes and regulations on investors.

Financial Architecture

The debt problem in the industrialised world has raised questions about the desirability and viability of a world economy whose chief currency is the US dollar. It raises questions about the entire post–World War II financial architecture, in which the rules of the game and the institutions have been created and defined principally by the United States. *Financial architecture* refers to the system of rules and institutions that form the foundation on which commerce and financial markets operate.

Geopolitics arises when states begin to attack or abandon the existing financial infrastructure, as we see today with the concerted efforts of China and Russia to create alternative institutions and currencies to compete with the system that has dominated the world economy since World War II. Similarly, geopolitics arises when the United States and western European nations seek to exclude a country, such as Russia, from the global financial and trading system.

The World Order and Finances

These characterisations of a world order are relevant to an investor or fund manager because they affect prices, markets, and valuations. A central characteristic of geopolitics today is disagreement about the current world order. China, Russia, and other emerging markets are no longer content to submit to the current world order. Investors must now ask themselves what will happen to the United States' ability to continue spending beyond its means if Russia, China, and others no longer believe that financing the gap between the United States' income and its expenditures is in their own interest.

To put this issue in perspective, the Congressional Budget Office estimated in 2014 that the United States will go from paying $233 billion annually in interest payments alone to $880 billion, thus making interest costs one of the largest items in the US budget—surpassing defense spending and Medicaid and dwarfing all other expenditures except Social Security and Medicare. Therefore, the movement toward more transactions in renminbi or rubles instead of US dollars is not just a technical economic issue. It is a means of allowing a sovereign the freedom to finance its own expenditures—or depriving a sovereign of that freedom.

In contrast, a nation that depends on foreign investment and foreign-supplied assets, like food, can find itself isolated and unable to grow in the absence of outside capital—as Argentina, Russia, and others have discovered when they have either chosen to default or decided to restrict the ability of foreign investors to buy or sell assets within their borders.

The geopolitics of finance raises important market questions. Does it matter to markets, prices, and valuations if core global commodities like oil and food are no longer priced in US dollars? What power does being a "reserve currency" really confer? Another way of looking at this question: Perhaps the true definition of a superpower is a state that the world's investors continue to fund even though it spends beyond its means, tampers with currency stability, and overreaches geopolitically.

Seigniorage

The global financial architecture matters to pricing and valuation in the financial markets. It matters whether oil and other critical commodities, including food, will be priced in US dollars or renminbi. It matters whether the rules of the game are defined by the United States or by China and Russia. The country whose currency is the reserve currency has the privilege of paying back debt in its own currency. It has the power to simply print money, which also brings the added advantage of something called *seigniorage*. This word derives from the phrase "the power of the lord to mint money." The *Financial Times* defines seigniorage as the "revenue governments derive because the cost of minting coins or printing paper money is less than the market value of that money." To lose this privilege of seigniorage is to lose the freedom to spend more than one earns without incurring a penalty from the market (usually in the form of relatively higher interest rates).

Russia, China, and others now envisage a world economy with a new set of rules and without the same dependence on the United States—on its currency or its philosophy and global institutions—as in the past. They also envisage a United States that loses its reserve currency status and thus incurs much more discipline from the markets. The *cost* of having reserve currency status is that the nation with that status tends to build up a trade deficit owing to the relative strength of its currency.

Others, mainly in emerging markets, believe that the efforts of central banks to create inflation (QE) should be viewed as hostile acts because the consequences—higher food and energy prices—cannot be easily addressed by domestic monetary policy responses. A rate hike in India will not bring down the global price of food nor will it produce more protein.

So, the potential for social unrest, which a higher cost of living inevitably incites, fully justifies some nations in their efforts to reach across borders for such critical assets. People need food and energy at the right price or they will turn on their government. Therefore, QE warrants not just an economic policy response but also a military response. The logic: If you default on us (and inflation is just a form of default), we are justified in protecting ourselves by any means, including reaching across borders for critical assets—from food supply chains to energy assets to strategically valuable territory. Whatever the driver or the logic, commodities have always been a potent source of conflict and geopolitics throughout history.

Pax Americana

The current world order (Pax Americana) is based on the post–World War II financial system. This system was initially called Bretton Woods, after Bretton Woods, New Hampshire, where a meeting was held on 1–22 July 1944, before the end of World War II, with delegates from the United States' allies in the war—the winning side. The delegates agreed to a broad infrastructure that would form the philosophy, principles, and practical means of conducting trade, commerce, and finance in the postwar world.

The simple idea behind the Bretton Woods system was that there should be relatively free movement of goods, people, and capital across borders. In other words, markets, rather than states, should determine the allocation of wealth in the world economy. At the time of its creation, the Bretton Woods system clearly sought to be a counterpoint to Communist ideology, which put the power to allocate wealth, assets, and even jobs into the hands of the state.

Initially, this postwar financial system was based on a loose gold standard. Instead of pegging the value of currencies directly to gold, the Bretton

Woods system pegged the value of currencies to the US dollar, which was defined as 1/35 of an ounce of gold.

This system worked well until the United States began to experience inflation in the late 1960s and early 1970s. At that time, Robert Triffen, a Belgian economist, became famous for identifying the "Triffen dilemma"—namely, that the United States was obliged to have a permanent trade deficit if it wanted to provide the world with the US dollars other countries needed, given that everything was priced in US dollars. This dynamic created an "overhang" in which the US trade deficit got worse and the global demand for US dollars increased. Politically, the United States became less comfortable with the situation. The seemingly permanent trade deficit to which such a system gave rise did not sit well with US voters.

In addition, during this period, starting in the early 1960s, the United States "overspent" by attempting to have both "guns and butter"—the idea that a state should spend on both war and social programs that raise the quality of life for its citizens. The United States committed to the Great Society programs that President Johnson hoped would help integrate the African American population into the mainstream economy and society. Johnson also sought to win the ever more costly war in Vietnam while spending more on the weapons needed to maintain a balance of power with the Soviet Union. In other words, he accelerated a nuclear arms race with the Soviet Union.

The combined cost of all this proved too great. Inflation began to creep up in the mid-1960s, and by 1971, President Nixon believed that he had to choose between preserving the Bretton Woods system and preserving the US standard of living. Naturally, he chose to support the interests of voters and announced that the United States would leave the gold standard, devaluing its currency and thus risking further inflation (which ensued and remained a problem until after the end of the decade).

This action meant that foreign investors in US and US dollar–denominated assets suffered a sudden fall in the price and value of those assets. Other countries experienced weaker growth because the devalued US dollar made US goods and services less expensive and thus more attractive. The decision to leave the gold standard meant that the United States was able to restore its competitiveness at the expense of others in the Bretton Woods system. In response to complaints that the United States was inflating—effectively defaulting on its creditors and undermining the Bretton Woods system—John Connally, secretary of the Treasury at the time, famously said in 1971 that the US dollar was "our currency and your problem."

This background is important today because Russia and China now believe that they have had to live with a global financial architecture that was designed by the United States to serve US interests but that has not necessarily served their interests as well—or even well at all.[9] The Federal Reserve's attitude seems very similar to John Connally's. The Federal Reserve either denies that QE has any spillover effects or argues that emerging markets should take responsibility for such effects and act locally to manage price stability. This view is a modern version of "our currency, your problem."

As the United States and the G–7 have stumbled into ever-larger debt problems and financial imbalances, Russia and China have been at the forefront in the creation of a new, alternative financial architecture. At one level, this is a technical exercise that involves the creation of new institutions—such as the BRIC Bank, in which China, Russia, and many other emerging markets have pooled their reserves and made mutual commitments to support one another in times of instability.

This effort involves moving the pricing and valuation of transactions away from US dollars and toward rubles and yuan. It also involves changing the current balance of power in existing Bretton Woods–era institutions, such as the IMF, the World Bank, and the UN. In each case, China and other emerging markets want a greater voice and more voting power on the basis of their increased financial commitments to each institution.

The competition to control or dominate the global financial architecture has intensified. The United States and Russia have increasingly turned to financial market and economic sanctions as they argue over the geopolitics of both Ukraine and the South China Sea. The United States continues to ban China from access to high technology while offering China's rival, India, full access to the highest technology of all: its nuclear program. This is economic diplomacy and a "sanction" of a different sort. The United Kingdom has proposed that Russia be banned from using the SWIFT (Society for Worldwide Interbank Financial Telecommunication) settlement system, on which global banking depends to execute money transfers from one bank to another and from one country to another.

It is not only nations that need to consider whether the old financial architecture of Pax Americana still serves their interests. Investors have many reasons to rethink the existing world order when they see a European nation like Cyprus expropriate privately held assets, as it did when so requested by

[9]It is worth noting that one of the central difficulties in thinking about geopolitics is that states do not "feel" nor do they usually have one view. A policy position may be established, but even within a single government, there will typically be several different points of view on any given issue. However, there is usually a sense of *zeitgeist* (literally, spirit of the time), a general public or policy preference that becomes known if not assumed.

the very institutions that form the heart of the global financial system—the EU, the World Bank, and the IMF.

The G–8

Another element of the financial architecture is the cornerstone of the effort to create an ongoing dialogue between the most important economies, popularly known, until recently, as the G–8 gathering of major economic powers. The G–8 is now back to being the G–7 because of Russia's departure from the group. Initially, in 1975, it was the G–6. Canada joined in 1976, thus creating the G–7. In 1998, it became the G–8 when President Clinton formally invited Russia to join the group. In 2014, Russia renounced its participation in the G–8 over the Ukraine issue. In contrast, frustrated by their lack of a strong voice, the emerging markets pushed for the creation of a similar group that could confer on economic issues: the G–20.

6. Statecraft and National Interest

No study of geopolitics can occur without some awareness of the concepts of national interest and statecraft. National interest is defined by the values, principles, goals, and objectives that a nation pursues in the belief that doing so serves its citizens. Statecraft is the means by which these national interests are pursued.

National Interests

According to the Commission on America's National Interests (in July 2000), "Vital national interests are conditions that are strictly necessary to safeguard and enhance Americans' survival and well-being in a free and secure nation." The commission then outlined these interests.

Vital US national interests are to:

1. Prevent, deter, and reduce the threat of nuclear, biological, and chemical weapons attacks on the United States or its military forces abroad;
2. Ensure US allies' survival and their active cooperation with the United States in shaping an international system in which we can thrive;
3. Prevent the emergence of hostile major powers or failed states on US borders;
4. Ensure the viability and stability of major global systems (trade, financial markets, supplies of energy, and the environment); and
5. Establish productive relations, consistent with American national interests, with nations that could become strategic adversaries, China and Russia.

Instrumentally, these vital interests will be enhanced and protected by promoting singular US leadership, military and intelligence capabilities, credibility (including a reputation for adherence to clear US commitments and even-handedness in dealing with other states), and strengthening critical international institutions—particularly the US alliance system around the world.

Extremely important national interests are conditions that, if compromised, would severely prejudice but not strictly imperil the ability of the

US government to safeguard and enhance the well-being of Americans in a free and secure nation.

Extremely important US national interests are to:

1. Prevent, deter, and reduce the threat of the use of nuclear, biological, or chemical weapons anywhere;
2. Prevent the regional proliferation of WMD and delivery systems;
3. Promote the acceptance of international rules of law and mechanisms for resolving or managing disputes peacefully;
4. Prevent the emergence of a regional hegemon in important regions, especially the Persian Gulf;
5. Promote the well-being of US allies and friends and protect them from external aggression;
6. Promote democracy, prosperity, and stability in the Western Hemisphere;
7. Prevent, manage, and, if possible at reasonable cost, end major conflicts in important geographic regions;
8. Maintain a lead in key military-related and other strategic technologies, particularly information systems;
9. Prevent massive, uncontrolled immigration across US borders;
10. Suppress terrorism (especially state-sponsored terrorism), transnational crime, and drug trafficking; and
11. Prevent genocide.

National interests can conflict and often do. The fact that both the United States and China now define some or all of the South China Sea as an area of "core interest" sets them on a confrontational path. Similarly, the desire by both the EU and Russia to encourage Eastern European nations in their respective directions sets these two entities on a path to conflict.

Investors must determine the pricing and financial consequences when a state or territory leans one way instead of the other.

The Instruments of Statecraft

Statecraft is the art of leading and governing a state in the pursuit of national interests. States are trying to achieve their national interests at all times, so this is the defining aspect of their behaviour. But the definition of national interest, as outlined earlier, can change over time and from one government to another. Priorities shift within the agreed-on definition of national interest in ways that also affect markets.

If power and sovereignty are indivisible, then all tools are at the disposal of the sovereign in its pursuit of the national interest and conduct of statecraft, however these may be defined. Geopolitics then requires study of the tools. Here is a short list of the tools that investors should keep in mind when analysing geopolitics:

- Influence and prestige
- Diplomacy (commercial, political, cultural, and economic)
- Espionage and intelligence gathering
- Enforcement, both domestic (police function) and international (military function)
- Taxes, tariffs, fines, levies, and expropriation (price controls, inflation, asset seizure, unannounced or unlegislated tax increases)
- Military tools
- Political, cultural, and commercial tools
- Methods of conducting geopolitics

Geopolitics, as a word, has a hard edge to it. It tends to suggest that relations between or among nations are not going well. Otherwise, the more neutral language of commerce and international relations would be deployed. Even the word "diplomacy" implies that there is a difference of opinion, a dispute that somehow must be managed in an effort to prevent geopolitics and conflict. So, it is worth considering the various facets of geopolitics and thinking about how to price the risk associated with them.

For Thomas Schelling (1960), the Nobel Prize–winning economist and political scientist, this field of study was not "geopolitics but rather the 'strategy of conflict'":

> Among diverse theories of conflict—corresponding to the diverse meanings of the word "conflict"—a main dividing line is between those who treat conflict as a pathological state and seek its causes and treatment and those that take conflict for granted and study the behavior associated with it.

Whatever the driver—bad actors or bad rules—conflict is inherent in geopolitics. There would be no need to project power if there were no conflicting goals, views, and beliefs. The purpose of power projection is to change the situation beyond one's own borders.

Sovereign Wealth Funds and Geopolitics

Sovereign wealth funds present important issues for market investors and sovereigns alike. An SWF is a pool of capital established and managed by a country for its own benefit and typically invested abroad. The central purpose of an SWF is often to prevent accumulated excess capital and reserves from driving up inflation or causing economic imbalances. An SWF is a mechanism for pushing reserves outside the country while still serving national objectives. The apparent goal of an SWF's investment program may be to secure the best possible return on capital. But in the main, SWFs are not driven by performance alone. They usually also serve to further such national interests as obtaining access to strategic assets and resources, from food to technology.

SWFs have worked very hard to diminish the world's attention on their geopolitical role and goals. Instead, they have emphasised their investment strategies from a performance perspective. This tactic worked well in a world where geopolitics did not dominate the global landscape. Investors feel great safety in following, or even front running, SWF investment strategies and make immense efforts to try to secure investment mandates from these large institutions. After all, their sheer size means that any investment is likely to be significant and potentially market moving. As a result, SWFs have also tried hard to keep the breadth of their interests/operations and their investment strategies relatively secret. The reappearance of geopolitics on the global investment landscape will make this strategy more difficult to manage. **Figure 5** depicts a cartogram of world countries resized according to their estimated GDP and purchasing power parity for 2015.

Ted Truman (2010, p. 2), in his landmark book on the subject, *Sovereign Wealth Funds: Threat or Salvation?*, pointed out that SWFs are

> symbolic of two major, recent trends in the global political economy: (1) a redistribution of wealth and economic and financial power from the United States, Europe, and other mature industrial economies to countries perceived to be less firmly grounded in similar economic, financial, and political mores; and (2) an increasing role of governments in managing wealth and economic power.

This description is no longer exclusive to the new emerging markets. The advent of government intervention and quantitative easing has blurred or moved the line between government and market in the industrialised world.

Figure 5. Cartogram of Total Estimated GDP Measured in Purchasing Power Parity, 2015

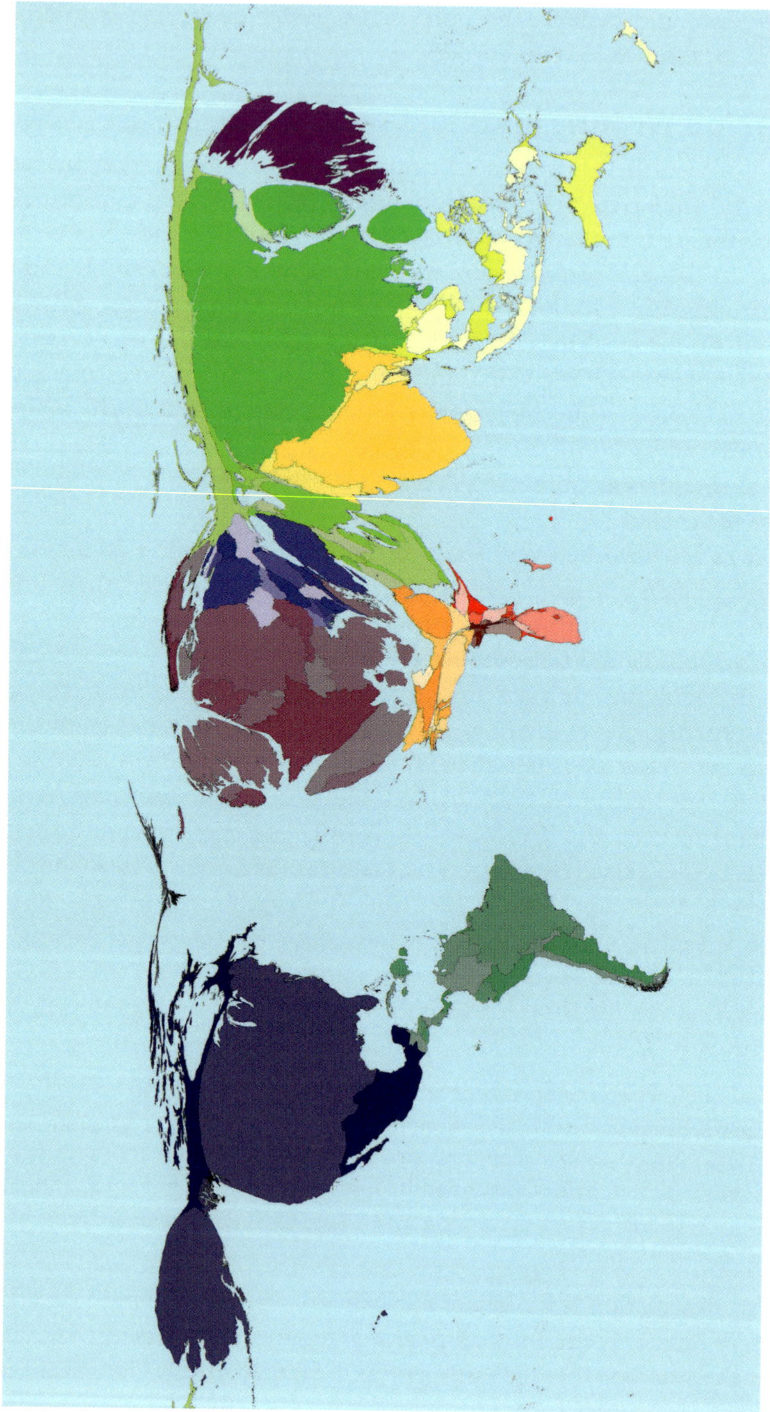

Source: Copyright www.worldmapper.org. Reprinted with permission.

Robert Jenkins, a former fund manager who served on the Financial Stability Board at the Bank of England, has pointed out that QE alone results in such an enormous accumulation of excess reserves that it becomes nearly impossible for a central bank to actually sell the sovereign debt it holds without disrupting the sovereign debt market and the economy at large. Thus, central banks have created the conditions under which they accumulate reserves as large as those of an SWF, which they cannot sell. In 2013, Jenkins wrote, "Markets are mesmerised by how and when central bank policies will be unwound. But they should also consider the possibility that such policies may not be unwound at all."[10] In other words, central banks may have inadvertently become SWFs or taken on some of their characteristics.

The fact that the United States, the United Kingdom, Japan, and others have emerged as the largest market buyers of their nations' debt instruments means that investors cannot easily short these markets. These governments have also actively used moral suasion and, sometimes, financial repression to compel private sector fund managers and investors to hold more sovereign debt than they otherwise would have. Financial regulation increasingly makes other banking and asset management practices—including proprietary trading, short selling, and the use of complex derivatives—more difficult.

State Intervention

It would be easy to assume that nations with SWFs have a higher degree of state involvement in the economy. But with governments in indebted countries playing such a large role in markets, it has become appropriate to ask, Who has more state intervention and central planning now? This is an important question in a world where geopolitical motives can be ascribed to many investment actions. Many emerging-market governments view QE in the developed world as an effort to default on them and to export inflation. Developed-country governments find it increasingly difficult to distinguish between a nation's political stance and its investment activities. It would be hard to imagine, for example, that Russia's SWF could attempt to buy an asset in the United States or the United Kingdom while simultaneously forcing US and UK fighter jets to scramble in response to air incursions. Or, in a less dramatic example, it becomes easier to imagine nations being disinclined to see national food production assets fall under foreign control, especially when the value of such assets is increasing.

[10]Robert Jenkins, "Swiss Example Questions Need for QE Unwinding; the SNB Has Laid the Foundation for a Sovereign Fund," Markets Insight, *Financial Times* (29 May 2013).

Critical Assets

There are, of course, formal methods for determining whether a foreign nation, or one of its entities, should be permitted to buy "critical" assets. For example, the United States has the Committee on Foreign Investment in the United States, which the US Treasury describes as "an inter-agency committee authorized to review transactions that could result in control of a U.S. business by a foreign person ('covered transactions'), in order to determine the effect of such transactions on the national security of the United States." Australia has its Foreign Investment Review Board, which, according to the Treasury, undertakes to "examine proposed investments in Australia that are subject to the Policy, the *Foreign Acquisitions and Takeovers Act 1975* (the Act) and supporting legislation, and to make recommendations to the Treasurer and other Treasury portfolio ministers on these proposals." Most nations have some sort of mechanism for vetting foreign ownership of critical assets or assets deemed to have some aspect of national interest attached to them.

Modern Warfare and Diplomacy

Investors fear the greatest instability that can occur in markets: war. Investors are also generally uncomfortable with diplomacy because it can involve negotiating away valuable assets without clear compensation. When investors are given a choice, however, diplomacy beats war.

Civil strife and war remove all certainty as to who is in charge. Nobody knows who owns what or whether an asset is safe. War destroys the social contract. It undermines all investment activity except for the provision of wartime needs. No one wants war and no one wants to talk about it until it is under way. Even then, there is an inclination to deem a conflict insignificant if it is localised.

But the fact is that wars continue to occur, and it is worth considering how much their conduct has been changed by technology and how much it remains the same as before. **Figure 6** illustrates the military budgets of the world's nations; the area of each country in the cartogram is drawn in proportion to that country's military budget (converted into US dollars at purchasing power parity). After the United States, the dominant military powers are China, Russia, a number of European countries, India, and Saudi Arabia and several other Middle Eastern countries.

Figure 6. Cartogram of World Military Expenditures

Source: Copyright www.worldmapper.org. Reprinted with permission.

Technology and Warfare

Technology has changed the ways in which war and diplomacy are conducted just as it has changed everything else. There are many examples of traditional "boots on the ground" combat, such as the ongoing wars in Iraq, Afghanistan, and Syria. But ever more subtle and sophisticated methods are being used.

Cyberwarfare. Rather than fight an opponent in a direct contest, these days many states prefer to simply disable their opponents' weapons or weapon systems. Preventing action is a less costly strategy than destruction.

The private sector is drawn into the geopolitical realm of cyberwarfare all the time. Staff members are spied on by competing governments that seek to glean information about deals, assets, intentions, and national security goals. Telecommunication companies have been compelled to hand over data on private conversations—or have been spied on by those seeking the same data.

Banks, investors, fund managers, and policymakers alike are key targets in the geopolitical game of asset acquisition. Some hackers are after a payout or even ransom. Others simply want access to the chatter. But the idea that only governments are after data no longer holds true. In the past, governments had their offices swept for listening devices as a matter of course. Today, private firms need to be nearly as vigilant. Commercial espionage is a central geopolitical issue for investors.

Both governments and investors have concerns about the vulnerability of critical infrastructure (e.g., the power grid) to cyberattacks. It would be hard to imagine that an investor in US electricity grids could remain ignorant of the many efforts by governments and hackers alike to turn off the grid, electronically or otherwise.

Sophisticated Weapons. Investors tend to assume that the various nuclear and ICBM treaties that were negotiated during the Cold War are still in place. Sadly, there is a new arms race. The United States, Russia, Japan, China, India, and others are all experimenting with or perfecting weapons that have a greater capacity to inflict damage than ever before. Hypersonic missiles now cut the delivery time of a nuclear or conventional weapons payload to such an extent that the so-called red line that connects Washington and Moscow or Beijing and Tokyo by phone could scarcely be used before it was too late.

Space-based electromagnetic weapons are capable of inflicting severe damage to infrastructure while leaving any survivors confused as to what happened. In May 2014, a US U-2 spy plane flying over California inadvertently "fried" and shut down the air traffic control system at Los Angeles International Airport, revealing that such powerful magnetic emissions can halt operations on the ground.

Near Catastrophes

In June 1999, it is now believed, India and Pakistan came within minutes of setting off a multiple warhead nuclear exchange. The so-called Kargil Crisis of 1999 was seemingly averted only by the patient diplomacy of President Clinton. Obviously, such an event would have had a material and negative effect on financial markets and asset prices, not to mention the environment. But most investors would consider it a "three- or four-standard-deviation event." In other words, the probability would be so low and the impact so high as to warrant ignoring the risk altogether. But when such catastrophic events actually occur, such as 9/11, investors respond immediately.

Outsourcing Conflict

A very important trend has re-emerged in recent years. Nations are increasingly outsourcing their defense and military activities to external parties. The rise of such entities as Blackwater (now called Academi) and other private military companies reflects a number of trends. First, nations have insufficient funds to pursue conflict directly. Second, outsourcing the activity is seen to help with outsourcing the blame. Third, using external private parties permits a degree of plausible deniability. Finally, outsourcing avoids the unpopular use of young draftees and volunteers with few practical alternatives to military service. Arguably, almost every major nation has outsourced to private entities the pursuit of its national interests and national security, to one degree or another. Although some may argue that the word "mercenary" does not apply to the modern use of external parties, it is clear that throughout history, nations have paid not only their own soldiers but also private soldiers to advance their cause.

Insourcing Conflict

Some investors, as well as military forces, have noted that there seems to be more social tolerance of Special Operations conducted by highly trained professionals than of ordinary "boots on the ground" soldiers. In the past, geopolitics may have required armies and a great deal of sophisticated equipment. Today, a Special Ops officer can do as much damage, or more, by inserting a virus-laden thumb drive into a computer—which means that it becomes harder for investors to know when a "war" has begun.

7. Practical Applications

It is fascinating that investors and fund managers tend to believe that price movements in the market are mean reverting but do not seem to assume that geopolitics tends to mean revert as well. Typically, when a market-moving geopolitical event occurs, it initially appears as a surprise until a glance at history reveals the event's long roots. For example, border disputes tend to be long-standing rather than spontaneous. Ancient rivalries continue to express themselves over time. Britain has long been a reluctant partner with continental Europe, so it should be no surprise that questions about the benefits of participation in the EU linger there. Spain and Greece have had such bad experiences with dictatorships and war that their citizens may be willing to endure more pain from their economic weakness in the EU than might otherwise be probable. All of Eastern Europe has found itself torn, at some point, between its political aspirations to belong to the West and its strong economic and cultural ties to Russia. The Middle East has a long-standing tendency to fall back into ancient tribal disputes. Can it really be a surprise, for example, that Turkey asserts itself more aggressively in the region given what we know of the Ottoman Empire?

There are plenty of investors who believe that a random walk, "monkey with a dart" approach will outperform the active investment management industry. They become index fund investors. But as an industry and a profession, fund management tends to assume that there are patterns of behaviour in markets rather than just random walks. Many, if not most, investors place value on active management and on the knowledge needed to engage in it. Therefore, drilling down into geopolitics, as one of many drivers of price movements, makes sense. But for those who believe that geopolitics matters—and who accept the fiduciary responsibility to find and benefit from profit opportunities while guarding against unnecessary losses—the question is, what is the right approach?

Is Expertise Required?

The sudden return of geopolitics to the global investment landscape required many investors to suddenly seek the counsel of "experts" on Ukraine or the South China Sea or ISIL and its caliphates. It is interesting to note that few fund managers would consider a couple of phone calls with an "expert" on a company proper due diligence for making an equity investment in that company. But they will take that approach when it comes to geopolitics.

This state of affairs may be due to the heavy reliance on math and algorithms that contributed to the demise of what used to be called "country risk" officers or experts. The entire function became outmoded when the peace dividend and the great moderation of inflation, together, pushed up the value of emerging markets and drove down the risk of political interference. This explanation makes sense. In a world where markets are growing, there is less need to argue about how to divide the spoils. Even if the spoils are not evenly distributed, the belief that many might share in future prosperity encourages people to carry on with work rather than waste time arguing about political control. For politicians, prosperity provides a platform for promises, for future benefits that shore up their support.

Indexation and benchmark investing also played a part in killing off the need for geopolitics and country-risk experts.

Reliable growth also meant that the risk of default and expropriation seemed to have receded from the investment landscape in the post–Cold War years. Many people have made fun of Walter Wriston, the late CEO of Citigroup, who famously said in 1982, "Countries cannot go bankrupt." Note that he did not say that Citigroup invested on the belief that countries could not go bankrupt. He said it some years after the Latin American debt crisis had occurred, when the ongoing pain of debt repayment was so great that it became clear countries might need to "declare bankruptcy," as a company can, in order to clear their debts and start their economies anew. In fact, this was the idea behind the famous Brady Plan in 1989. Brady bonds were collateralised with US Treasuries and effectively permitted defaulted emerging-market nations to re-enter the capital markets. The Brady Plan was one of the most important geopolitical events of its era.

Similarly, in 1994, the Mexican peso crisis was resolved when the United States provided a loan (which Mexico collateralised with future oil revenues). These kinds of government-sponsored solutions are examples of power projection. The United States and the industrialised world sought to contain the economic and political deterioration among the Latin American nations by providing loans to protect the interests of their own investors and nationals. But the intervention also further reduced the risk that geopolitics would destroy value.

So, what is the right approach for systematically addressing geopolitical risk?

Big Data

Investors love to quantify risk, so they will inevitably be drawn to *big data* as a means of detecting geopolitical events and forces. The approaches that investors take range widely—from keyword searches on Twitter that can detect social unrest before the media can to the volume of phone calls emanating from a location. The effort to find reliable signals has been going on for a long time. It was not that many years ago that hedge funds deployed spotters near the White House to observe late-night pizza deliveries. The more pizzas and the later the delivery hour, the bigger the problem. These simple observations continue today. In June 2014, local plane spotters detected the arrival of two US B-2 Stealth bombers (apparently with the call signs Death 11 and Death 12) and three B-52 Stratofortress aircraft at the Fairford Royal Air Force Base in the United Kingdom, just west of London. Such aircraft are normally based in the United States, so their arrival prompted a flurry of commentary on the internet. Not all the relevant data are necessarily "big."

But big data will provide more and more information about geopolitical events and trends, making it easier for investors to be aware of what is happening. At the very least, this tendency reduces the chance of unpleasant surprises.

Outsourcing

One approach is to outsource the subject of geopolitics. Some professional investors will simply reach for the phone whenever a geopolitical event occurs and get a handful of experts to brief them. This common approach might be called "occasional outsourcing."

It is interesting that no serious investor would take this casual approach to the actual assets they are buying and selling, such as equities, hard assets, or debt instruments. This approach assumes that the central investment strategy or themes can only be marginally affected by geopolitical events. The purpose of acquiring information is to appear knowledgeable quickly. At best, such an approach assumes that the investment strategy is essentially sound but that it can be marginally tweaked if geopolitical events or forces are serious enough.

Another approach is to outsource the subject of geopolitics in an ongoing way: "ongoing outsourcing." Investors can hire outside experts to serve as "radar" and to be alert to any signs or signals that geopolitics is beginning to affect market prices. The drawback to outsourcing, even the ongoing kind, is that the investor also has to disrupt or modify existing investment strategies in order to accommodate new geopolitical events. The implicit assumption is that geopolitical events are rare and that geopolitics even more rarely requires any adjustment to the investment strategy.

Think Tanks and Lobbyists

Washington, DC, is probably the world's capital of think tanks and lobbying, though they exist worldwide. Think tanks are usually nonprofit organisations. They are groups of policy experts who typically remain very close to policy making in hopes that they will enter or return to government positions.

The problem with think tanks, from a market perspective, is that most of them are not very market oriented. They are good at providing the history of a geopolitical dispute or event. They are good at providing a nuanced view of the current state of the dialogue on geopolitical issues. They are not typically very good at translating what such events mean for the markets. Nor are think tanks "neutral." They tend to lean to one end of the political spectrum or the other, although there are some exceptions. They also rely on funding by both governments and private firms, and so institutional bias is an issue.

Lobbyists are another group that often serves as a resource to investors. Lobbyists, by definition, have a specific agenda. They represent a client and are obliged to pursue that client's objectives. So, a lobbyist will represent a nation like Pakistan or Argentina and a particular policy objective, such as promoting a public relations agenda. Although lobbyists can be very well informed, the presence of this underlying commercial interest must be kept in mind.

Unlike occasional outsourcing, ongoing outsourcing implies a continuing dialogue that increases the chances that geopolitics will be incorporated into the strategy in a more continuous fashion.

Either way, outsourcing is costly. It may be that some geopolitical events do not move markets, and so there will be criticism of the decision to spend.

Open Sourcing

Banks and asset managers used to employ country-risk officers. But increased confidence in the speed and efficiency of algorithms and mathematical model–based investing reduced the need to have live personnel involved in the asset allocation process, especially those who might focus on obstacles and risks rather than opportunities. The situation in the asset management industry somewhat mirrors the decision taken in the intelligence community in recent decades to focus on high-tech, algorithm-based intelligence at the expense of (human) intelligence officers on the ground.

Some might argue that the intelligence community is spending the combined GDP of many nations on its intelligence gathering and still not getting it right all the time. Therefore, it would be pointless for an investor to try to replicate such a costly effort. But it is interesting to note that intelligence communities increasingly rely on "open source" information—that is, they prefer to use information that is already in the public domain and not classified in any way. In fact, intelligence communities have begun to incorporate market intelligence into their efforts to gather and process information.

This development is partly a function of the World Wide Web and modern technology. Think about what George F. Kennan said in 1997, when he testified before the US Senate at an intelligence hearing. Deputy head of the US Embassy in Moscow from 1944 to 1946 and author of the famous "X" article in *Foreign Affairs* in 1947, which strongly shaped US policy toward the Soviet Union for a generation, Kennan said:

> The need by our government for secret intelligence has been vastly overrated. I would say that something upwards of 95% of what we need to know about foreign countries could very well be obtained by the careful and competent study of perfectly legitimate sources of information open and available to us.[11]

It is fascinating that intelligence and defense agencies increasingly seek to bring in market experts to help fill out their understanding of geopolitical risk and market investors increasingly seek to align themselves with defense and intelligence community experts for the same reason. The varying perspectives make for a more robust assessment of the risk factors. As a small example, during the last decade, the financial community held a strong belief that the middle class in China would not only grow but also form the basis for strong internal investment in China. The defense and intelligence community, in contrast, mainly focused on the deteriorating demographic picture in China and asked, *what* middle class? Obviously, these two opposing perspectives resulted in two very different investment strategies.

Insourcing

KKR, the private equity firm, has created a foundation called the Global Institute, with a prestigious board of directors, that is clearly aimed at securing geopolitical insights and advantages. Commercial firms have done something similar, creating or hiring think tanks to provide insights and expertise on geopolitics. The Hong Kong trading house Li & Fung, for example, created the Fung Institute. Many companies are backers of the Council on Foreign Relations in the United States, Chatham House in the United Kingdom, and their local equivalents internationally in hopes that this support will provide access to geopolitical intelligence.

[11]Daniel Patrick Moynihan, *Secrecy: The American Experience* (New Haven, CT: Yale University Press, 1998): 227.

This insourcing approach affords investment firms access to the best of both open sourcing and outsourcing options. It gives them an internal advisory board at their disposal. It gives them a network of experts and active policymakers who are directly involved in the geopolitical issues of the day. But they also have the benefit of an external network. For KKR, its foundation serves the following purpose:

> Anticipating, understanding, and knowing how to respond to emerging geopolitical and macro-economic trends as well as the impacts of revolutionary technological changes are critical to smart investing, portfolio management, and risk mitigation.

Asset Acquisition

The founder of Amazon, Jeff Bezos, is a former banker and an active manager of his own wealth. Arguably, one reason he decided to purchase the famed *Washington Post*, the main newspaper in Washington, DC, is that it is probably the least expensive and most effective method for garnering cutting-edge information about politics, policy, and geopolitics. After all, the *Washington Post* staff have unparalleled access to policymakers, to experts who are jockeying for the opportunity to write op-ed pieces, to whistleblowers, and to those who want to leak information. It is, in effect, a far less expensive method for gathering information than paying the lobbyists in Washington for their insights or paying for any other outsourcing option. Almost everyone who matters will volunteer information to the editorial board of the *Washington Post*.

In another example of insourcing and acquisition, Shell, the oil company, created a division that engages in scenario planning in 1972. Shell Planning's reputation as a horizon-scanning group is legendary. It does not pretend to predict the future, but it has found that thinking about possibilities better prepares the firm for the expected and unexpected alike. According to Shell Planning, "Scenarios give us lenses that help us see future prospects more clearly, make richer judgments, and be more sensitive to uncertainties."[12] The fact that Shell Planning is an internal division means that it has an ongoing voice in the company's strategy. It is not a reactive function. It is designed to help Shell get "in front of" geopolitical developments and even anticipate them with greater accuracy and certainty. Others will argue that the share price of Exxon, for example, has outperformed Shell's over the years, so the scenario planning at Shell, as an overhead cost, has not been worth it.

[12]See "40 Years of Shell Scenarios, 1972–2012" (http://s05.static-shell.com/content/dam/shell-new/local/corporate/corporate/downloads/pdf/shell-scenarios-40yearsbook080213.pdf).

Special Situations

One final option is to put in place a team whose primary job is not only to find historic dislocations but also to put capital behind them when they occur. This option would be the very antithesis of benchmark investing. Such an approach probably requires providing a pool of actual capital as an inducement and encouragement to find profitable geopolitical events. A special situations philosophy assumes that the existing assumptions about the nature of the state, the social contract, and the geopolitical landscape are potentially wrong. For example, a benchmark fund manager might underweight sovereign debt if the assessment was that the sovereign's ability to repay the debt was impaired. A special situations approach might consider what would happen if a state's ability to repay was genuinely impaired. Which assets would be privatised or nationalised? Which deals or companies might cease to exist or come into existence? Which nations might cease to exist or come into existence?

For a special situations approach to succeed, the investor would need not only capital available (probably on short notice) but also an ability to operate across asset classes. The Brady Plan, which was deployed in the Latin American debt crisis, involved debt equity swaps. The US loans to Mexico during the peso crisis were collateralised by future sales of oil reserves.

8. Conclusion

Investors inevitably must balance risk and reward. Some risks are four-standard-deviation events that are too expensive to hedge or insure against even if they can be anticipated. Geopolitics has the capacity to bring risks and opportunities, both large and small, onto the investment landscape. The question is, How much time and effort can be devoted to this particular task? Prediction is nearly impossible, but preparedness is attainable and desirable. Fund managers and investors need to ask whether preparedness is best achieved through scenario planning, by including geopolitics as one of many drivers of the actual investment strategy, or by changing the investment team or the information sources and services that the team uses.

As always, markets represent diverse interests and abilities. Some will find a way to add geopolitics to their investment scenarios and to profit from it. Others will take comfort in knowing that they were only one of many investors to utterly ignore geopolitics. But at least now, with this book, there are some core ideas about how to think about the subject. These ideas may prove useful as geopolitics returns to the investment landscape ever more forcefully.

References

Agnew, J.A., and S. Corbridge. 1989. "The New Geopolitics: The Dynamics of Geopolitical Disorder." In *A World in Crisis? Geographical Perspectives*. 2nd ed. Edited by R.J. Johnston and P.J. Taylor. Oxford, UK: Blackwell.

Al-Rodhan, Nayef. 2012. *Meta-Geopolitics of Outer Space: An Analysis of Space Power, Security and Governance*. London: Palgrave Macmillan.

Angell, Norman. 1910. *The Great Illusion: A Study of the Relation of Military Power in Nations to Their Economic and Social Advantage*. London: Heinemann.

Brzezinski, Zbigniew. 1997. *The Grand Chessboard: American Primacy and Its Geostrategic Imperatives*. New York: Basic Books.

Carr, E.H. 1939. *The Twenty Years' Crisis, 1919–1939: An Introduction to the Study of International Relations*. Reissued with an introduction by Michael Cox. New York: Palgrave, 2001.

Cohen, Saul. 2009. *Geopolitics: The Geography of International Relations*. 2nd ed. Lanham, MD: Rowman & Littlefield (originally published in 2002 as *Geopolitics of the World System*).

Dodds, Klaus. 2007. *Geopolitics: A Very Short Introduction*. Oxford, UK: Oxford University Press.

Fukuyama, Francis. 1989. "The End of History?" *National Interest*, vol. 16 (Summer): 3–18.

Hawtrey, R.G. 1930. *Economic Aspects of Sovereignty*. New York: Longmans, Green & Co.

Hooson, David. 1966. *The Soviet Union: A Systematic Regional Geography*. London: University of London Press.

Howard, Michael. 1994. "The World According to Henry: From Metternich to Me." *Foreign Affairs*, vol. 73, no. 3 (May/June): 132–140.

Huntington, Samuel. 1993. "The Clash of Civilizations?" *Foreign Affairs*, vol. 72, no. 3 (Summer): 22–49.

Kaplan, Robert. 2012. *The Revenge of Geography: What the Map Tells Us about Coming Conflicts and the Battle against Fate*. New York: Random House.

Kennedy, Paul. 1987. *The Rise and Fall of the Great Powers: Economic Change and Military Conflict from 1500 to 2000*. New York: Random House.

Kissinger, Henry. 2014. *World Order.* New York: Penguin Press.

Luttwak, Edward. 1990. "From Geopolitics to Geo-Economics: Logic of Conflict, Grammar of Commerce." *National Interest*, vol. 20 (Summer): 17–23.

Mackinder, H.J. 1902. *Britain and the British Seas.* New York: Appleton.

———. 1904. "The Geographical Pivot of History." *Geographical Journal*, vol. 23, no. 4 (April): 421–437.

Mahan, Alfred Thayer. 1890. *The Influence of Sea Power upon History, 1660–1783.* Boston: Little, Brown.

Schelling, Thomas. 1960. *The Strategy of Conflict.* Cambridge, MA: Harvard University Press.

Truman, Edwin M. 2010. *Sovereign Wealth Funds: Threat or Salvation?* Washington, DC: Peterson Institute for International Economics.

Wallerstein, Immanuel. 1974. *The Modern World-System. Vol. 1, Capitalist Agriculture and the Origins of the European World-Economy in the Sixteenth Century.* New York: Academic Press.

Yankelovich, Daniel. 1972. *Corporate Priorities: A Continuing Study of the New Demands on Business.*

RESEARCH FOUNDATION CONTRIBUTION FORM

☑ **Yes**, I want the Research Foundation to continue to fund innovative research that advances the investment management profession. Please accept my tax-deductible contribution at the following level:

Thought Leadership Circle................ US$1,000,000 or more
Named Endowment..................... US$100,000 to US$999,999
Research Fellow .... US$10,000 to US$99,999
Contributing Donor....................... US$1,000 to US$9,999
Friend .... Up to US$999

I would like to donate $ ____________________.

☐ My check is enclosed (payable to the Research Foundation of CFA Institute).
☐ I would like to donate appreciated securities (send me information).
☐ Please charge my donation to my credit card.
☐ VISA ☐ MC ☐ Amex ☐ Diners

Card Number

___/___
Expiration Date

____
Name on card PLEASE PRINT

☐ Corporate Card
☐ Personal Card

____
Signature

☐ This is a pledge. Please bill me for my donation of $ ____________
☐ I would like recognition of my donation to be:
☐ Individual donation ☐ Corporate donation ☐ Different individual

____
PLEASE PRINT NAME OR COMPANY NAME AS YOU WOULD LIKE IT TO APPEAR

PLEASE PRINT ☐ Mr. ☐ Mrs. ☐ Ms. MEMBER NUMBER ____________

Last Name (Family Name) First Middle Initial

Title

Address

City State/Province Country ZIP/Postal Code

Please mail this completed form with your contribution to:
The Research Foundation of CFA Institute • P.O. Box 2082
Charlottesville, VA 22902-2082 USA

For more on the Research Foundation of CFA Institute, please visit www.cfainstitute.org/learning/foundation/Pages/index.aspx.

Named Endowments

The CFA Institute Research Foundation acknowledges with sincere gratitude the generous contributions of the Named Endowment participants listed below.

Gifts of at least US$100,000 qualify donors for membership in the Named Endowment category, which recognizes in perpetuity the commitment toward unbiased, practitioner-oriented, relevant research that these firms and individuals have expressed through their generous support of the CFA Institute Research Foundation.

Ameritech
Anonymous
Robert D. Arnott
Theodore R. Aronson, CFA
Asahi Mutual Life
Batterymarch Financial Management
Boston Company
Boston Partners Asset Management, L.P.
Gary P. Brinson, CFA
Brinson Partners, Inc.
Capital Group International, Inc.
Concord Capital Management
Dai-Ichi Life Company
Daiwa Securities
Mr. and Mrs. Jeffrey Diermeier
Gifford Fong Associates
Investment Counsel Association of America, Inc.
Jacobs Levy Equity Management
John A. Gunn, CFA
Jon L. Hagler Foundation
Long-Term Credit Bank of Japan, Ltd.
Lynch, Jones & Ryan
Meiji Mutual Life Insurance Company
Miller Anderson & Sherrerd, LLP
John B. Neff, CFA
Nikko Securities Co., Ltd.
Nippon Life Insurance Company of Japan
Nomura Securities Co., Ltd.
Payden & Rygel
Provident National Bank
Frank K. Reilly, CFA
Salomon Brothers
Sassoon Holdings Pte. Ltd.
Scudder Stevens & Clark
Security Analysts Association of Japan
Shaw Data Securities, Inc.
Sit Investment Associates, Inc.
Standish, Ayer & Wood, Inc.
State Farm Insurance Company
Sumitomo Life America, Inc.
T. Rowe Price Associates, Inc.
Templeton Investment Counsel Inc.
Frank Trainor
Travelers Insurance Co.
USF&G Companies
Yamaichi Securities Co., Ltd.

Senior Research Fellows

Financial Services Analyst Association

For more on upcoming Research Foundation publications and webcasts, please visit www.cfainstitute.org/learning/foundation/.

Research Foundation monographs are online at www.cfapubs.org.

11326144R00046

Printed in Great Britain
by Amazon.co.uk, Ltd.,
Marston Gate.